BETWEEN THE LINES

By Debbie Gibson

with Mark Bego

DIAMOND BOOKS ◇ Austin, Texas

This is dedicated to my family, friends, and fans for their continued support.

— Debbie Gibson

Photo Editors: Deborah Gibson, Mark Bego, Linda Sanfilippo and Diane Gibson
Cover Photo: Kevin Mazur
Interior Photos: The Deborah Gibson Collection
Chris Cuffaro
J. Michael Dombrowski
Dave Jones
Kevin Mazur
Allen Olivo
Werner Roelen
David Salidor
Thomas Schuman
David Tan
Albert Watson
Art Director: Mark Bego

FIRST EDITION

Published in the United States of America
By Diamond Books
An Imprint of Eakin Publications, Inc.
P.O. Drawer 90159 ◇ Austin, TX 78709-0159

ISBN 0-89015-735-9

Contents

Introduction

As an entertainment industry author and journalist, I am often invited to attend performances by up and coming new singers. I remember in March of 1987, being invited to attend a party and a late night performance by a sixteen-year-old singer named Debbie Gibson, at a club in New York City called "1018." I recall thinking to myself, "What is a sixteen-year-old girl doing singing love songs in a nightclub that she isn't even old enough to get into?" and "I wonder if she is going to be any good?"

I met Debbie that evening, and all the members of her very friendly and supportive family. I distinctly remember being charmed by Debbie's warm and confident manner; however, I was still a little skeptical about what I was soon to witness on stage.

When it finally came time for Debbie's performance, I was totally blown away! Not only did she sing and dance with professional confidence and ease, but her refreshingly "up" and positive personality came across sincerely in each of her memorable and original songs. That night I became an immediate Debbie Gibson fan.

Since that time I have closely followed Debbie's career, and I consider her a valued friend. Over the past three years I have had the privilege of attending several of the important events in her career, including photo sessions, video shoots, private parties on Long Island and at the Hard Rock Cafe in Manhattan. One of my favorite moments came on the opening night of her three-day engagement at Radio City Music Hall in the fall of 1988. When Debbie made her entrance that night, I was standing in the audience next to her parents, Diane and Joe. It was very exciting for me to see the combination of pride, love and supportive energy that mirrored in their eyes as they watched their eighteen-year-old daughter entertaining a cheering, sold-out crowd of ecstatic fans.

Debbie's career has grown in monumental strides since that time. She has continued to produce hit after hit, including "Only In My Dreams," "Foolish Beat," "Out Of The Blue," "Shake Your Love," "No More Rhyme" and "Staying Together." In March 1989 her album "Electric Youth" and her hit single "Lost In Your Eyes" both sat in the Number One spot on the music charts in *Billboard* magazine. And with the single, "Lost In Your Eyes," Debbie became the youngest person to have ever written, produced and performed her own Number One hit! (She beat Stevie Wonder's claim to that distinction in the 1960's with "Fingertips, Part II.") Debbie's debut album, "Only In My Dreams" sold over three million copies, and "Electric Youth" is likewise on its way to becoming Triple Platinum.

It was in early 1988 that Debbie and her mother and I discussed the possibility of collaborating on a book. Well, at long last, here it is: *Between The Lines.* The following text you are about to read is direct from Debbie to you, in her own words. We spent many hours at her house in Long Island, discussing every detail of her fascinating career, and she revealed several never-before-published stories. Most of her fans don't realize that she was in the film *Ghostbusters,* appeared with Placido Domingo in *La Boheme* at the Metropolitan Opera, and had a successful career in television commercials, before she became a singing star. We talked about school, boyfriends, fashion, songwriting, her family, her friends, her room, and her upcoming film career.

Not since Stevie Wonder and Michael Jackson has there been a teenage singing star like Debbie Gibson! While writing her own page in music industry history, Debbie Gibson and I have put her memorable life story down on paper, and I hope you enjoy it. I'm certain that you will be as fascinated by Debbie's outstanding creativity and enchanted by her sincerity and charm, as am I.

— Mark Bego
New York, 1989

1

Hello, My Name Is Deborah

Picture a top music executive sitting in his office. A twelve-year-old girl and her Mom knock on his door. He opens the door, and the girl says, "Hi, my name is Deborah and I write songs, and I have a demo I'd like you to hear. Here's my picture and resume. I've done theater and commercials and . . ."

"Sure, O.K. kid, thanks," and he slams the door. Well, that's exactly what happened to me!

It would have been easy to just accept that and walk away — but I didn't. It happened over and over again, but who cared? I knew I was going to make it — with or without these people . . . it was just a matter of time. I was that confident about my music, and determined to succeed.

Let me introduce myself. I'm Debbie Gibson, and basically, I consider myself a singer/songwriter. I'm nineteen years old, and my life is very normal — except for one small detail: I'm in the spotlight! That does change my life a bit, but I try to not let it change it *too* much. I still know what's important. What's important, really, is: family and friends, and just basically having fun and being happy.

I would definitely say that I'm a normal nineteen-year-old, in the sense that I like to do things that every nineteen-year-old does. A lot of people see me dealing with the adult side of the music business, and they think that I'm older than I am. But they don't realize that the young side of me is still very young.

Although I work very hard on my music, I don't think of making records as a job or a business, because it's what I love to do, and what I've always loved to do. It's just always been my hobby — and my first love. A lot of people might think that one night I decided to kind of go into this business to make money, and to become famous. Obviously, there were never any TV cameras rolling when I was in my living room, just sitting there playing piano for hours on end. You don't get paid to do that, either. I think you just have to really love it, and I really do.

Even more than songwriting, I would have to say that performing is my first love — above everything else. And, even more than that I love performing the songs that I have written. Because I have done a lot of theater, I've obviously performed other people's work, but there's much more satisfaction involved when I'm performing something that I have come up with myself. Introducing something new to the world is much more exciting for me than just performing something that everyone's already heard.

Although I am still basically the same Deborah Gibson I always have been, suddenly being considered an internationally known pop singer changes several aspects of your life. In some ways it makes things easier for me. In other ways, it makes things more difficult. Sometimes it makes everything more fun, but there are other times that it puts a lot of pressure on me. It's a little bit of all those things.

The stardom part of it definitely makes it more fun, because it's nice to know that when I'm writing a song, it's going to go further than just my living room. It's nice to know that I'm going to have the opportunity to perform it in front of thousands of kids and see their reaction. At the same time, there's a lot of pressure involved. I put a lot of pressure on myself, because I like to do everything myself. The reason for this is that I like everything that I do to be the most honest representation of me that it can be. I don't want to be packaged and put together and styled.

I know what I like. The artists that I admire are like that, too. They're just very true to themselves, and that's how I am. So, I do put a lot of pressure on myself. People tell me to delegate responsibilities to others once in a while, but I have a hard time doing that.

Because of my busy schedule, my typical day is quite a hectic one. Right now I am in the midst of putting together a show to take on

tour. Here's what my days are structured like at the moment: First, I get up. Some days I go to the nutritionist, because I'm on a special diet now. I think all the hamburgers, Chinese food, and pizza from the last year kind of caught up with me, and I found myself lacking energy at times. I've learned that you have to eat right if you really want to keep going. But, I have to confess: I still love junk food!

I've been rehearsing with a choreographer lately, so I will dance for, say, three to five hours, and then I will drive over to rehearsal. Sometimes afterward, I might go to a movie or something, then I will come home, and maybe hop on the phone.

I do have some time to myself, and one of my favorite things is to stay up really late at night. Because my work day doesn't usually end until late at night, I'll stay on the phone and write songs, and things like that, until really late. I also like to stay up and watch late-night television. I especially like to watch "Arsinio Hall" — I love that show!

A lot of people know me from just watching my videos, and in a way, the image of me on the television screen *is* a big part of me. But, let me describe myself: I definitely believe in having fun, and being silly. I think people can relate to that more than they can relate to someone who is slick and sophisti-

cated. I'm definitely not very sophisticated. I'm just a typical teenager; I'm pretty much of a mess!

I'm not really a homebody, in the sense that I like to sit home alone, but I don't really like the party scene. I don't like hanging out with strangers at a "chic" party, or stuff like that. I know what's real. I think I'm a very real person, and that I have very real friends. When we get together, we just kind of like to hang out and talk, and go to the movies, and stuff like that.

In a way, it's kind of strange for me to suddenly be looked at as a role model for other teenagers, but it goes along with being a performer. I think that once you're in any kind of position, whether you're a pop singer or an athlete, kids definitely watch what you do. What's good for me is the fact that I don't have any skeletons in the closet, and I'm exactly how I appear to be. And, I hope that I can influence kids in a positive way, and show them they don't have to go and do drugs to be successful in the music business.

My image is very much me. It's very honest. I think that my fans realize that, and it makes it easy for me to communicate with them. I really stay in touch with my fans through the letters they write to me. It's funny, because I answer as much of my fan mail as I can. But, I can only answer so much. When I sit down to write, I end up answering only a few letters at a time, because I might write each one of them a two- or three-page letter! I especially write long letters if someone's having a problem, or if I feel really obligated to help. Kids ask my opinion on things like I'm a friend — which is really nice!

I think that kids have picked up on the fact that I am very normal, and I like that because it also helps me. I'm mostly very independent, and I like getting in my car and going into town — even if I'm by myself — walking around. If people see you like that, then they don't get really hyper. They may come up to me and say, "Can I have your autograph?" or something. You can sometimes run into a problem, but for the most part, I think if you make yourself out to be a "celebrity," and you're surrounded by six big bodyguards, people are going to think of you as more untouchable. But, if you just act like yourself, then people are going to treat you more like a normal person. That is how I really want to be treated. I don't really want to be treated like a "celebrity" — ever.

A lot of stories that people read about me don't always portray me exactly the way I am. And a lot of interviews don't end up being in my own words. I really wanted an opportunity to show people exactly who I am. That is why I have written this book, so I can talk to my friends, one-to-one, and in my own words.

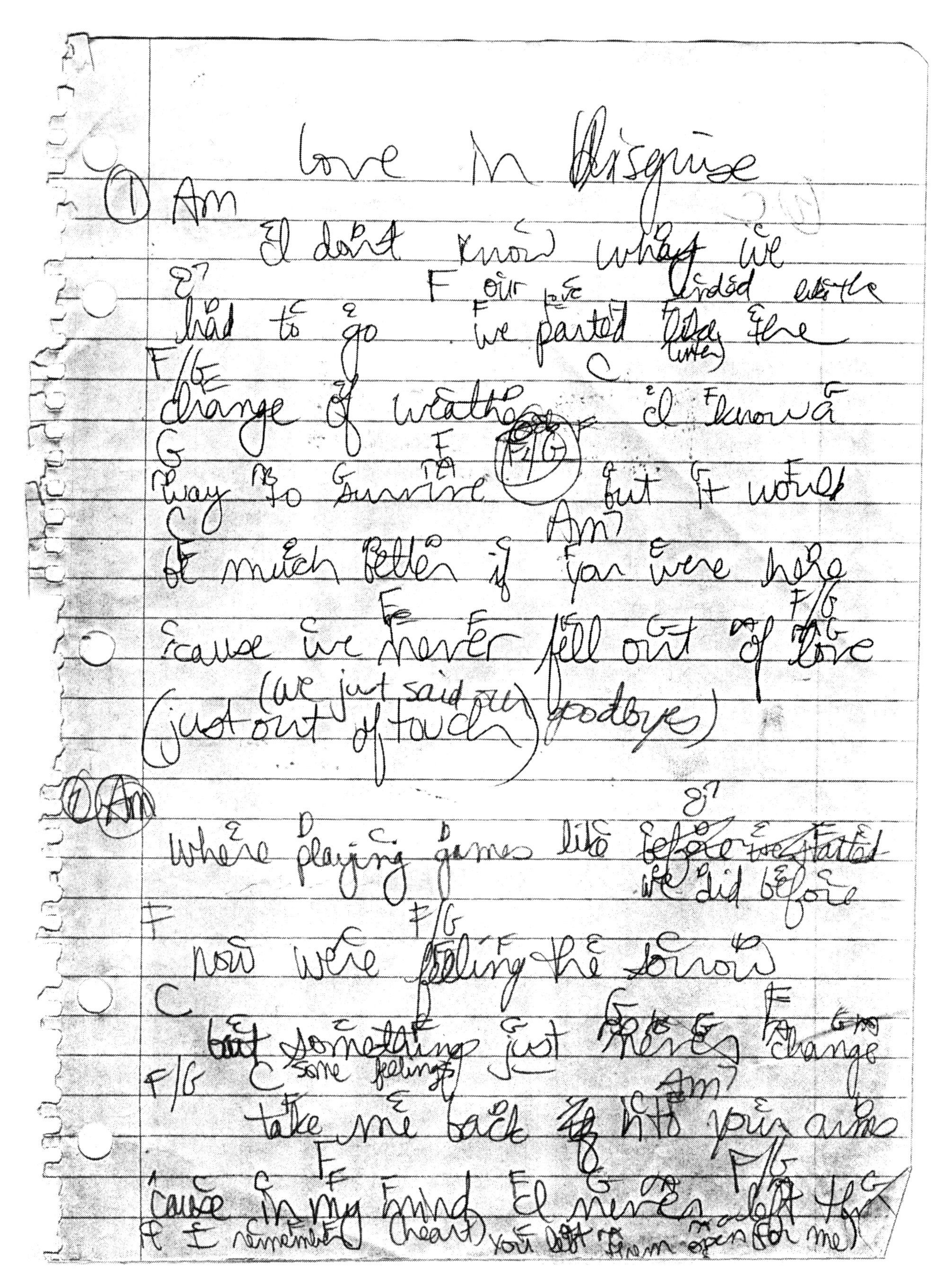
Love In Disguise

(1) Am

I don't know why we
had to go, we parted like the
change of weather. I know a
way to survive but it would
be much better if you were here
'cause we never fell out of love
(just out of touch) (we just said our goodbyes)

(1) Am

We're playing games like ~~before we parted~~ we did before
now we're feeling the sorrow
but something just never change
some feelings
take me back into your arms
'cause in my mind I never left

The original lyric sheets to the song "Love In Disguise," in my handwriting.

2

Shades of the Past

I was born in Brooklyn, New York, on August 31, 1970. I lived there, with my parents and my two older sisters, until I was two years old, when we moved to Merrick, Long Island. It was while we were living in Merrick that my younger sister Denise was born.

I'm the third of four girls: Karen is twenty-four, Michele is twenty-two, I'm nineteen, and Denise is fifteen. My dad works for an airline — in fact he's been working for an airline for twenty years now.

I don't remember the day that my family moved from Brooklyn to Merrick, but my mother's sister, Aunt Linda, to this day tells a very funny story about me and that particular afternoon. While my parents were busy moving all our things into the new house in Merrick, Aunt Linda decided that the most helpful thing that she could do was to watch my sisters and me. That way my parents could concentrate on the move, and we would be out of their way.

Aunt Linda decided to take me, Karen, and Michele to the beach for the day. The story that she tells is just an example of how I have always insisted on getting my own way! I guess I just drove her crazy the entire afternoon. She really had her hands full that day looking after three little girls. When we arrived at the beach at Reis Park, it was hot and crowded. Aunt Linda was trying to keep the three of us entertained, but I ended up being the most difficult one.

I had on my bathing suit, and I brought along a little metal folding chair to sit on at the beach, which I insisted on carrying. Unfortunately, at the age of two, I wasn't very good at carrying things, so I ended up dragging the metal chair behind me! According to Aunt Linda, the sound of me dragging that metal chair along the paved sidewalks of Reis Park sounded something like scraping your fingernails across a chalkboard. The sound was not only driving Aunt Linda nuts, but was also annoying to anyone within audible distance of me. Try as she might to get the chair away from me, I wouldn't let go of it until we found a spot on the beach to sit down. Everyone who could hear me was cringing!

After driving everyone on the beach crazy with my metal chair, when we finally sat down on the beach, I continued to insist on having everything exactly my way. My Aunt Linda was wearing a flowered cloth beach hat. I had a passion for hats even then, and I wasn't happy until I took it away from her, and insisted on wearing it the entire day. No matter what she did that afternoon, I had to have everything *my way*!

This little story is an example of how I

have always known exactly what I wanted to do, and how I have constantly found a way to achieve my goals — whether my goals were dragging my own chair along the sidewalk at Reis Park at the age of two, or recording and producing my own songs when I was sixteen. I laugh every time Aunt Linda tells the story of our day at the beach!

I don't know why, but I've always been into hats. I remember seeing pictures of myself as a baby, not only ones taken that day at the beach when I stole my aunt's hat and wouldn't give it back, but throughout my childhood as well. I even have baby pictures of myself when I was one or two, wearing things on my head. You know those crocheted things that people sometimes have in their bathroom which covers an extra roll of toilet paper? Well, we had one of those in our bathroom, and I have a picture of me wearing it on my head! It looked like a cute little hat to me! I also have pictures of me in a little satin cowboy outfit, and naturally, I had on a white satin cowboy hat to complete the "look."

One of my earliest memories is of Brooklyn. That's probably because my grandparents still live there. Right after we moved, I remember going to a "block party" in the summer. I can still recall the smell of Italian sausage and peppers frying, and of hot dogs and hamburgers. I remember going into one of the neighbor's houses, and just disappeared for a while. I was always independent, even when I was three! I nearly scared my family to death, but at the time I must have been thinking, "Oh, I think I'll go over to so-and-so's house now." I never even considered the fact that everyone would be looking for me!

Another of my earliest memories was definitely of the piano and playing the song "Billy, Don't Be A Hero." I remember running down the hall into my sister's room where the stereo was, listening to the song on the radio, and then running back to the living room, and playing it on the piano — by ear. A lot of people can pick out parts of a song, just with their right hand or their left hand. For me, that didn't sound like the record. So, I played with both my right hand and my left hand together — a kind of "oompah oompah" with the left hand. Those are my earliest memories.

Also, I asked for a guitar one year, for Christmas. I was two years old at the time. I don't even remember where I had seen a guitar. I asked for a guitar, but my parents figured it was too big, so I ended up getting a ukulele. Obviously, guitar was not my thing — nor was the ukulele — the piano always was.

We always had a piano in the house. My parents bought a piano even before they bought a couch. The piano was their first piece of furniture because they figured if they didn't just go ahead and get one, that they might not end up with a piano. They knew that they would eventually have to buy a couch, and they would find a way to buy a couch, so they would buy the piano first. They actually bought it first for themselves, because my mom always wanted to learn, and my dad — he was in a barbershop quartet when he was a teenager — so he was always very musical. Even though they really wanted it for themselves, they never got a chance to learn, because their kids monopolized it!

I played the ukulele until all the strings broke, and that was the end of my love of guitars. Actually, I eventually played the guitar again — in church, in a folk group. I could play a little bit when I was eight, nine, ten, and eleven. But you know what would happen? I didn't know all of the chords, and I guess I didn't have enough interest in it to put the time into it, so my older sister Karen played with me, and when I didn't know a chord, she'd play louder to cover up my mistakes for me!

I wrote a song when I was five, which my mom swears she's seen the music to around the house. I know it's here somewhere, but it's gotten mixed up in the shuffle when we moved. Anyway, it's called "Make Sure You Know Your Classroom."

My family lived in that house in Merrick from the time I was two years old, until 1988, when I was seventeen. Our house wasn't anything fancy, just a typical suburban ranch house. It wasn't really all that big, either. For a while, we had the bottom floor rented out. Downstairs was a TV room, a playroom where we kept all of our toys, and we used half of the garage as an extra room. Eventually it was turned into the TV room with a bed in it, for Michele, who was away at school. That way we all could have our own room. She just slept there when she came home. That half of the garage was turned into a den — and later it became my recording studio.

The upstairs had three bedrooms, and a kitchen and a living room. We had a piano upstairs and another one downstairs, because at one point, there were four of us taking piano lessons, and believe it or not — we used to fight over practicing! We were probably the only household in America where we actually fought over the pianos for practice time. That just goes to show you, when your parents don't force you to do something, and if you really want to do it — you'll do it!

I remember sitting there practicing classical piano when I was six, for three hours — and loving it! And I'd also sit there for another two hours playing popular music. I could always play by ear (which means that I can listen to a song, and play it on the piano without seeing sheet music in front of me).

The stereo was, of course, an important item in our house. When I was little, my sisters and I would dance around to such songs as "Breaking Up Is Hard To Do" by Neil Sedaka, "You'd Better Shop Around" by The Captain and Tennille, "Rubberband Man" by the Spinners, "Carwash" by Rose Royce, and "Rock Around The Clock" by Bill Haley and The Comets. We used to dance to those songs all the time. They were part of our record collection. Between listening to our record collection, and listening to the radio, it wasn't long before I fell in love with pop and rock and roll music!

I come from a very tight knit family. My parents were always very supportive of my musical aspirations, but they had their own. That meant they didn't always have time to drive me around to my lessons and other events. So, a lot of times my grandparents would take me to auditions and things like that.

My grandparents sat through EVERY school concert that I was in, and EVERY talent show, together with my Aunt Linda, my Uncle Carl, and all of my cousins. Those talent shows became a running joke in the family. First the overweight ballerina would come out and perform, and then the juggler would come out, and then the tap dancing troupe would come out, and EVENTUALLY I would come out on stage. Now that I think about, and consider the fact that my grandparents have six grandchildren, and what all they sat through at these talent shows, and what they STILL sit through — it's kind of funny! But they were always there, and always really proud and supportive.

My grandfather would sit for hours and listen to me play the piano. These were my grandparents on my mom's side of the family. My dad had been in a home for boys when he was growing up, so we don't know his side of the family at all. We only know Mom's side of the family: the Pustizzi's. It's a very Italian last name, and my grandparents' names are Josephine and Albert.

My family is a very close Italian family, even though my dad's part German. Because we didn't know his side of the family, basically we were raised as Italian/Americans. We would always go over to my grandparents house for great big Italian meals: the kind of meals where, just when you think that dinner's over — another course comes out! I remember all kinds of great Italian pastries like canoles and things like that. I grew up loving that kind of food. To this day, there's nothing like my grandma's and my mom's spaghetti sauce. That's probably the thing I miss the most when I'm on a long concert tour — is that sauce, because nothing comes close.

I hate Italian restaurants for that reason.

These photos were taken on the infamous "moving day" when I was two-years-old. Here I am dragging a chair at Reis Beach, and playing in the sand with Karen. I'm wearing my Aunt Linda's hat — which I refused to give back to her!

My Aunt Lena from New Jersey, once came to a show of mine at a college in New Jersey. She knew that I had been on the road for a while, and that I was missing that homemade Italian food, so she brought me spaghetti and meatballs. I just went crazy, I was so happy to have all of that great food!

My grandfather is one of thirteen kids, so we have what seems like a million relatives who live in New Jersey. They're all great, and age sixty-eight and up, and they're all really active on their farms. I think that's great. I hope that I've inherited their energy.

My dad was always very into music, and he would always sing to me and my sisters before we went to sleep. He'd play piano by ear, and was always like our "comic relief." He's a very fun dad. I used to dare him to audition for plays when I'd be auditioning for community theater shows. Once he did audition, and he got a part! I remember drilling him and going over and over his lines. He only had like five lines, but we'd go over and over and over them.

But he's great, and he has a great voice. In fact, he and I recorded "Have Yourself A Merry Little Christmas" on my 12-track recorder at home at Christmastime last year, and it was in "heavy rotation" on New York radio stations during the holidays. People were calling in and asking where they could buy the record, and meanwhile it was just this little demo that I had done with him. He sounds real good on it!

Last Christmas I got my dad one of those "You Sing the Hits" machines, so he could take out all of his musical frustrations on it. Now he can sing his own versions of things like the Frank Sinatra hits, and record them.

My mom has been very instrumental in

my career, and now she is my manager. In a sense, she always has been. We have always made decisions about my career together.

As parents, my mom and dad were always quite strict. But, they really raised us with good morals. I wouldn't change a thing about my childhood. My parents knew what was best for us, and they still do. I still trust their instincts about people. They were always the biggest supporters of me and my other three sisters — no matter what we wanted to do, they'd let us try it. Like, if I said, "Mom, I want to take gymnastics lessons," she'd say, "O.K., try it." Because, who knows, I could have turned out to be the next Mary Lou Rettin. You never know until you give a child an opportunity to find out what their "thing" is. Obviously, for me, music was it. But, my mom and dad never pushed us.

In our family, I'm the only one who is pursuing music as a career. My other three sisters aren't, even though they took piano lessons and all of that, it's just not what they wanted to do, and that's fine with my parents.

There are two molds in our family. For instance, Karen and I would be doing the dishes and singing, and my other sisters would be saying, "Would the two of you shut up! Why are you singing while you're doing the dishes?" Karen and I were always very much like that, and very into pop music. My sister Michele was into classical music and she was always more quiet. My sister Denise is kind of a combination of us. Denise is now very outgoing. She used to be incredibly shy. But, still she'd get up on stage, which was really funny. She has a really pretty voice, although she'll probably hate that I said it, because she doesn't really like to sing.

Michele and Denise are both into fashion. Denise is very quiet about things. They had an art show recently at her school, and the day before it, she said, "Oh, by the way Mom, some of my artwork is on display at school. Do you want to come to the show?" If I had artwork on display, I'd make sure that my entire family knew about it at least a month in advance and marked it down on their calendar!

Well, we went to the art show, and we couldn't believe how talented she really is! I'd never really seen her draw anything like that in my life. Mom was blown away! We all just have our own little things that we're into, and Denise is really into art and fashion designing, and so is Michele. In fact, Michele has done some of the styling on my videos, which is great, because I'm not very good with fashion. I can dress myself, but that's about it! I'm not visually oriented in that way. So, it's great to have my sister working with me like that. Also, she knows me better than an outside stylist would. It keeps it all in the family that way. If we can all work together that's the best thing, I think. It works out really well.

Karen now works for Atlantic Records. She worked first as an intern at Motown, and then at Polygram. At Atlantic she's doing A&R (Artist & Repertoire) work, and administering my publishing. She's enjoying herself so much. That's her thing. She loves the business end of the music world. It's great, because she knows so much about music. It's rare these days to be able to find people in the music business who really know about music. A lot of people are into the business, but she was always into the music as well.

It makes sense to me to have my family involved in my career. I trust my family more than I trust anybody. I had so much fun recently at the ASCAP Songwriting Awards. When I won my Award, Karen went up to the podium with me to accept the trophy, because both the songwriter and the publisher are honored at the ceremony. So, Karen and I went up to get the awards together, and it was so great, and so funny! We were going up to accept the award, and cracking up the whole time!

Karen recently got married, which is weird, because I still think of her as being too young to get married. Of all of my sisters, Michele is the sophisticated one. Karen and I are totally undomestic — we really don't cook and clean. And, Michele and Denise are real neat and organized — they can cook, and they can sew. So, it's kind of funny to think of Karen as married. When Karen got married, I knew she wanted a pet, so I arranged for her to get this dog through someone I knew. His name is Gulliver. He was a puppy at the time, but now that he has grown up, the thing is a terror! He eats shoes and things. Sorry about that, Karen!!

Karen and my new brother-in-law, Bill, handle my fan club magazine. Also, my grandfather and my dad work for the fan club. Bill puts the whole newsletter together, which is great, because I don't want to hand that over to a service, or to strangers. I think people like that rip off the kids who join fan clubs. For instance, my sister will call me up with the questions that the kids have written in to me, and I'll answer them. It's great like that, because it keeps it really personal.

When we were younger, my sisters and I appeared in several local stage productions together. I would always be trying to get them together for shows saying, "Let's do a show for Mom and Dad!" I'd boss everyone around. I'd want to direct it, and choreograph it, and be musical director! We used to put on little skits. I especially remember playing the *Grease* soundtrack album and performing to it. We never were into singing into hairbrushes, we were more into using real microphones! My Dad bought us a microphone for Christmas one year, when I was around eight years old. We used to plug that into the stereo, and make up little skits to the songs from *Grease,* and stuff like that. I used to make us little costumes and everything.

What used to be funny was when we went to auditions Karen would accompany me on piano when I sang, I would accompany Michele when she sang, Michele would accompany Denise when she sang, and Karen would accompany Michele. It was just the funniest thing! The accompanist used to see us coming, and go and take a coffee break! We were a really self-sufficient unit!

I remember going to Nunnleys on Long Island a lot as a kid. Anyone who grew up on Long Island, will remember Nunnleys. It's an amusement park with rides, and miniature golf. We have a lot of photographs from there. That used to be the favorite place to have birthday parties and stuff like that. Nunnleys recently closed, and I think that they're building condos or something in its place. Isn't that sad? It had been around since I was a little girl, in fact since before I was alive. It was so sad to hear that they were closing.

SCHOOL

In kindergarten we used to have what was known as "music hour." That was when a music teacher would come into the room, and we'd all sing. I loved music hour, and I would always get up in front of the class and sing. I remember one day my dad walked into the classroom, to bring me my lunch, which I had forgotten that morning, and there I was sitting up in front of the class, singing and playing piano. That was the day that I debuted my song "Make Sure You Know Your Classroom," to my kindergarten class.

I always used to get up in front of the class, and play and sing, and we'd have little singalongs. I used to stand up and sing "Michael, Row Your Boat Ashore" or "Old MacDonald Had A Farm." There was a piano in the classroom, and I was always playing it for the kids in my class.

I remember that once I got into trouble. There was this girl named Laura, and she lived down the block from me. We went to our first day of kindergarten together, and we both got in trouble, because we stood up and we were dancing again. She said, "This is your last chance." So she turned around, and we got up and began dancing again. There was a "bad table" that was set up for the kids who misbehaved. She sat Laura and I down at the "bad table," and I remember crying and crying. The teacher said to us, "As soon as you say, 'I'm sorry,' you can sit back at your own table." I remember that I couldn't bring myself to say, "I'm sorry," because I was crying so much. I couldn't seem to stop crying long enough to apologize. But, finally, I stopped crying enough so I could tell the teacher that "I'm sorry." For some strange reason, I remember that episode distinctly.

In school, I remember a chorus teacher named Dr. Wheeler, and another one named Mrs. Apostle. They were both great teachers. Dr. Wheeler retired, and then Mrs. Apostle came in and taught the chorus class. This was at Camp Avenue School, which was a public school in Merrick.

Throughout school, I was in chorus, and the band. In the band I played the flute. Also, for a couple of songs, I had to play the glockenspiel. Since I already played the piano, for me that was pretty easy. But, I had to march with the glockenspiel one year, carrying it — and it was kind of heavy.

I was in a program in fourth, fifth, and sixth grades, and it was called "WINGS." It stood for: "Widening Interests through New experiences for Gifted Students." That program was one of the things that I remember most about school. It was headed by a woman named Sheila Berman who is still running this program which has an accent on creativity. It is at Camp Avenue School, and Old Mill Road School, and Fayetteville School, in Merrick and in North Merrick. There are similar programs all over the area, but different schools have different ways of running it. What it does do is focus on creativity. You had to do an independent study, and you really had to research it. You had to include doing interviews and surveys, and reading books and everything that contributed to your area of concentration.

At the end of the program, you had to come up with an individual project, and you had to do a presentation. You would do your presentation in front of college professors, and you would get an evaluation. It was great. I remember one year I did "Pop Music" as my

Two of my publicity photos as a child actress. Now, I ask you: "Wouldn't I have been perfect for the cast of 'Annie?' "

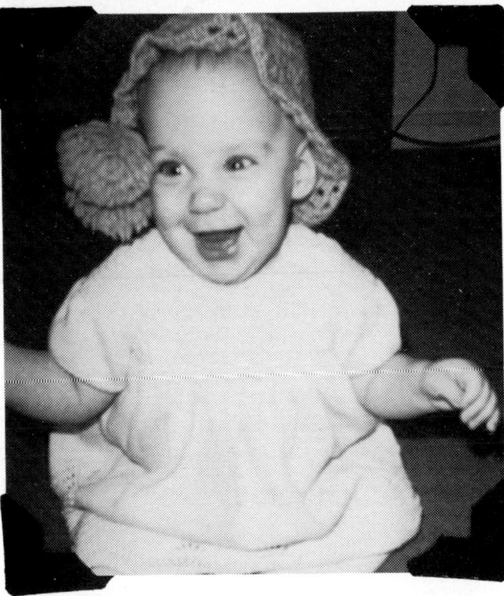

Me at six-months-old with a toliet paper cover on my head. I thought it was a cute hat!

At Disney World with Dad.

At two, at Michele's sixth birthday party.

My childhood in Brooklyn.

Playing "teapots" with my cousin Sal.

Karen's first Communion. That's me with the bouquet.

Just give me a hat and a tamborine and I'm happy!

Playing D.J. at my tenth birthday party.

With my grandparents at my first Communion, 1978.

Karen, Michele, Debbie, and Denise in "Sound of Music" at Cure of Ars Church.

In "Hansel and Gretel" at the Metropolitan Opera, 1982.

area of interest, when I was in fourth grade. I studied radio programming, and the hits and everything that were broadcast. One year I wrote an opera called "Alice in Operaland." What I did was, I took songs from various operas, and I bridged them together with my own songs. It was like Alice going through Operaland, meeting all these opera characters.

Another year my area of concentration was "Directing a Play." As my final project, I had to direct a play myself. I directed my own little "Best of Broadway." I had rehearsals at my house, and I made costumes. My sisters were the stage managers, and all of the technical parts. We gave the finished presentation at Old Mill Road School for the kids, like a school assembly. It went really well!

Also, as part of the WINGS program, we did a mini-study, which was a topic that the whole class researched. We also did "Creative Problem Solving," which consisted of being presented with a problem, where you would have to brainstorm as a class, and then you would come up with a solution to it. That was part of a whole national competition, and our team placed third in the nation that year! That was a really incredible experience. One of the WINGS teams, this year, 1989, did the same thing.

This past spring, I went back to the school and talked with the kids, and kids are studying subjects like "acid rain," the death of John F. Kennedy, and all sorts of really serious subjects. And these kids are nine and ten years old! But, if you give the kids an opportunity to do things like that, you'd be amazed at what they come up with. I mean, you need the academics that come out of books, but I think that the WINGS program helped me become an independent thinker and problem solver — more than any other program or class. If being creative is what you want to do with your life, then you need these experiences, and these types of situations to grow with.

In junior high school, I was in a gifted English student program, and my teacher, Dr. Deck, had us doing the same type of independent study projects. It was great!

With the WINGS program, you only missed a day and a half out of the regular school week, but you had to make up the work on your own time. You had to be quick to catch on. You had to take a test to get into the program, and a lot of the regular teachers didn't care for the program too much, because it took time away from the regular classes, but like I said, it sure helped me a lot.

This spring, when I went back to the school and talked to these kids, they asked me questions that are more intelligent and more in-depth than many of the questions that have been asked of me in interviews with professional journalists. I'm talking about real intelligent questions. These classes really taught intuitive thinking, as opposed to cut-and-dried subjects out of a book.

In the movie *Dead Poets Society,* that's what the film is about. Robin Williams says, "I thought that school is supposed to teach kids to think for themselves," because in it, his character is teaching at this really strict school. The other teachers in the school said, "Absolutely not, they must learn discipline. They must learn academics." The WINGS program was a little bit like that as well. It taught me to think for myself. It encouraged individuality.

When I was in school, I was always in the school plays. I played Cinderella in ninth grade. I was in *Fiddler On the Roof* in tenth grade, which was actually an excellent production. Unfortunately, at one point I lost my voice during the run of *Fiddler On the Roof,* and I really had to struggle through that one. I always wanted them to put on a production of *Grease* in high school, but they never did. I was so disappointed, because I had wanted to play Sandy. That was always one of my dream roles.

Throughout school I was a good student, as far as grades went. I had to be a good student, because I missed so much school for plays and auditions and things. The teachers couldn't stand my missing class, but what

This was my "composite head sheet" when I was a little girl. I appeared in several television commercials and films, including "Ghostbusters."

they couldn't stand more, was the fact that I would constantly do well. My mom always said to me, "If your school work ever starts to slip, I pull the plug on the singing, acting, and commercials." So, I just knew that I had to get good grades, and that was it. Somehow I had to do both the career, and the schoolwork, and I had to do well at both of them.

My first album, "Out Of The Blue," was released when I was in eleventh grade. So, when we were in the recording studio, taking a lunch break or a dinner break, I'd be doing my homework. The schedule was really hectic, and it was really, really hard, but I wanted to do it badly enough. And, if you want to do something badly enough, you're going to find a way to do it. I graduated from high school with a 92 overall average!

I do believe in academics as well, because I believe that to be able to have an intelligent conversation with someone, you have to have a little general knowledge. I confess that I was terrible in science, and I was terrible in social studies. And, I used to write songs in my social studies class all the time. In high school, my social studies teacher, Mr. Harrison was great. We would sit in a circle and talk, as opposed to just memorizing things from books. I learned a lot more about social studies than I would have if I had gone home and read the chapters in a text book. Mr. Harrison treated us like adults, which I think was really a good attitude.

That's the one thing that I didn't like about school in general, the fact that kids are often treated like they are idiots a lot of the time. I hate the idea of tests, too. Well, not the idea of tests so much, as the idea of getting graded for tests. In a way, you learn what you learn, and I never remembered anything that I *had* to learn for a test, because I memorized it the night before, and I forgot it the next day. To me, I just like absorbing what it is that I want to absorb. That's one of the reasons that I don't have plans to go to college. I want to take courses, and learn for myself, and not for a piece of paper at the end. I thought the whole idea of grades was silly. Obviously, there were some teachers whose tests were easy, and some teachers who gave tests that everybody failed. So, I tended to not really believe in the validity of tests.

Because of my schedule, I was constantly having to make up tests that I missed. I remember, at one point, I had like ten tests to make up at once! It was awful! I had one week to study for all of them. It was really hard, and my brain was on "overload," but somehow I pulled it off!

Looking back through all those years of juggling my schoolwork, my classes, and my music lessons, I can honestly say, "I wouldn't change a thing about my childhood!"

SA
adidas

DEBORAH GIBSON

3

Show Biz

I started taking formal piano lessons when I was five years old. At first my parents thought I was too young to take lessons, so Karen and Michele started a year before me. I badgered them enough, and finally I got to take lessons. We went to Anne DiAlto who was my first piano teacher.

One of the first things that I specifically remember is doing cartwheels behind the piano teacher's back! My sisters and I would go for piano lessons at the same time, and we'd all have to wait for each other. During my sisters' lessons, I remember doing cartwheels whenever the teacher turned her back! Then, I would quickly sit down, just as she'd turn around because she thought she'd seen someone back there. I distinctly remember doing that.

I also remember that while I was waiting for my sisters to take their lessons, the teacher's mother would give me sewing lessons. I always liked to make things, like little pillows. And, she taught me to knit. That's how I used to pass my time between piano lessons — waiting for my sisters.

During the first year of lessons, all I would do is sit and listen to my sisters practice, and the piano teacher would give me the same pieces which I played by ear. I fooled her into thinking I could read the music. I'd stare at the page of music, and I'd play the piece. Then one day, she pulled the book away and realized that I wasn't reading the music. I did it for a year and got away with it! So, I had to go back to the beginning, and I had to learn to read music.

The first piece that I learned in music class was Beethoven's "Für Elise." That was for a CYO (Catholic Youth Organization) talent contest, at Sacred Heart Church, where we went in Merrick.

I won first place in the contest. But, the funniest thing is, I knew I was going to win. A couple of other people had played the same piece in the contest, and they played it kind of choppy. Because the one thing that my piano teachers were really great with was playing with dynamics and expression — above everything else. I remember that when the other people played the piece before me, they played it really stiff and choppy, and I kept saying to my mom, "That's not right. They're not playing with feeling! I'm gonna win, I'm gonna win!"

When it came time to announce the winner, the announcer said, "First Place is . . .", and I didn't even wait for them to say my name. I just stepped out of my seat before they even said my name, and my mom was sitting there dying of embarrassment, going:

"I hope she won or this is going to be even more embarrassing!" Fortunately, I won! I was always a little over-confident I guess, which I think has helped me. I'd rather be like that, than ever be unsure of myself.

I did my first play when I was seven, and that was *The Elves and The Shoemaker,* at the Town of Hempstead Repertory Theater. It was really the "teen" repertory theater. Again, I said, "Oh, I may as well go and audition — what the heck?!" So I did, and I got a part. So did Michele and Karen — we were three of the Elves.

The next play that I appeared in was *The Sound of Music,* and that was with Denise and Karen and Michele — we were cast as four of the seven kids. One of the boys who was in that production was Tommy Williams, who is now my lead guitarist!

I remember my audition for *The Sound of Music* very well. I sang "New York, New York," because I used to love to belt those high notes. That was one of the auditions where we all took turns playing piano for one another. That was one of the best shows that I've ever done. It was so well put together. That was at Cure of Ars Church, also in Merrick.

Tommy and I didn't get along at this point, because we both wanted to be in the spotlight. We both wanted to be playing the piano. I remember once, the director bought me helium-filled balloons for my birthday, and Tommy went and popped them all. We were total rivals. He'll kill me for telling this story, but I've told it a million times! One day at rehearsals, Tommy climbed into a trunk, and he was just playing around, so I snuck up and locked it on him. I turned it on its side, and sat on it, and he was banging on the inside of the trunk trying to get out. People were passing by, saying, "Have you seen Tommy? It's time for his rehearsal." And I said, "No, I haven't seen him. I don't know where he is." So, that was revenge for me. I had gotten back at him, and we still laugh about that episode today.

Tommy is really, really talented. It's so funny to think that he grew up to become the lead guitarist in my band! Now, we get along fine.

Also around the time of *The Sound of Music,* I was auditioning for the Broadway production of *Annie.* That was a big thing in my life. This was about 1977, and it was for the second or third cast of *Annie.* I auditioned for that show about ten times, because I was so determined to be in it.

For the first audition, I dressed totally wrong, because I wore a cute pink dress for this role where you had to look scruffy. I couldn't believe how some kids dressed for that audition — like they were already playing the roles! Some came in wearing an Annie wig, and the red dress like the cartoon character wore. Some of them came looking like orphans — all dirty. A lot of that was because their parents dressed them up like that — which is really a bad move. The song that you had to sing for that audition was "Happy Birthday." That was the first song that you had to sing, and if you could pull that one off you might get to do "Hard Knock Life" or "Tomorrow." I'm so sick of the song "Tomorrow." I have heard it so many times in my life, and I sang it so many times. At the "Annie" audition, you'd hear it sung for what seemed like five thousand times! It was ridiculous. One time I got down to the ten finalists, and they were choosing a company for the road, for the national touring company. They were choosing five kids. So, they had us in two groups, and it came down to basically one group of five or the other. It was for four of the orphans, and the understudy for Annie. It was between me and another girl for one of the roles. I knew that I was too tall, but I always went to the auditions anyway. They wanted midgets! You had to be four-foot-six or shorter, and I was four-foot-seven. So, I used to wear baggy pants, and I'd bend my knees so I wouldn't look an inch too tall! Well, someone went by and tapped all of our knees, and suddenly I rose above the rest of the group. That was the end of that. I didn't get the role because I was too tall.

Then, I was cast in the same role in a

AGENT____________

AGE RANGE_______

DEBORAH GIBSON
AEA / SAG
ASCAP

HAIR: Light brown / blonde
EYES: Hazel
HEIGHT: 5 ft 5 ins.
WEIGHT: 95 lbs

SIZE: 5/7 Junior
VOICE: Soprano/Alto

CREDITS

RECORD RELEASE

"I Come From America" For International Release
Lyrics and Music By Deborah / Recording Artist

COMMERCIALS
VOICE OVERS

For National Advertising Agencies
(List upon Request)

STAGE

A Christmas Carol / Sheldon Harnick....Belinda
Nozze De Figaro... Operaworks.....Barberina
Harrison Loves His Umbrella.......Town Hall
Metropolitan Opera Childrens Chorus
Hansel & Gretel, La Boheme, Le Rossingol
Annie..............................July
Mickey & Friends Part II...........Broadhollow Th.
Gypsy....................Baby June / Louise
Annie Get Your Gun................. Little Jake
The Sound o Music.................. Marta
South Pacific......................Ngana

FILMS

Ghostbusters........................Day Player
Book of Daniel........................Day Player
Aetna Industrial.....................Principal
A.A.A. Industrial.....................Principal

RADIO

Ray Heatherton Show
WOR Radio

TELEVISION

Joe Franklin Show
Fame
La Boheme / Hansel & Gretel (Live from The Met)

SHOWCASES & CLUB ACTS

Int'l Games for The Disabled / Zachareys & Reception
Something Different
American Dental Assoc...........World Trade Center

TRAINING

Acting & Speech.................Showcase Studios
Piano............9 years.. M. Estrin
Voice............3 years.. T. Arrigo
Dance.. Tap/Jazz/Modern....Phil Black / Gregg Burge
Guitar/Flute/Gymnastics/Musical Theater

SPECIAL RECOGNITION

WOR Songwriters Competition (age 22 yrs & under)..1st place
N.Y.S. Songwriters Competition.....1st place
Annie.........Top 10 Finalists Broadway Company
N.Y. Music Scholorship Assoc. / All County Choir

SPECIAL SKILLS

"PERFECT PITCH" Sight Singing, Sight Reading
COMPOSER / LYRICIST (songs & jingles)

This was my acting resume when I was twelve-years-old. As you can see, I've always kept very busy as a singer and as an actress.

non-Union company production of *Annie.* Unfortunately, since I'm a member of the Union, again I couldn't appear in *Annie.* I was so upset. I didn't care where I did it, I just wanted to do that role. I eventually did appear in a local production of *Annie.* I played one of the orphans in the show at the Broadhollow Theater in Farmingdale.

The other shows that I performed in included productions of *South Pacific* at Sacred Heart Church and Hofstra University, and *Cinderella* at the Town of Hempstead Teen Repertory Theater. In that production of *Cinderella,* I was too young for any of the parts in the script, so they simply wrote in a role for me, as the Fairy Godmother's Helper. I was supposed to be invisible. Only the audience could see me, and the Fairy Godmother. It was really funny.

I used to love doing theater. I would do that instead of going to summer camp. I loved doing plays, and that particular theater group was great. Because you'd go for five hours a day, and you'd do improvisations and skits, and you rehearse, and you dance. Then you'd present various shows in the parks on Long Island, on a portable stage that they called The Showmobile. It was like being at camp. It was great! I loved it.

What I would usually do was appear with the Children's Theater during the day, and another theater production at night. Like at the same time I was doing *South Pacific.* I also did *Annie Get Your Gun* at Eisenhower Park, which was great, and was in front of thousands of people. That was really professional. As far as local theater groups go, that was probably the most professional one.

Probably my favorite role in my favorite play, is *Gypsy,* when I played Baby June. I did that when I was eleven or twelve, and that was performed at Calhoun High School. That was one of the best productions that I appeared in, and I just loved it. I could relate to that show a lot. Not from my own mother, but just from going on auditions and seeing "stage mothers" going into that, "Sing out Louise . . . smile baby!" routine that they do from the wings. I have heard and witnessed so much of that, that it became a joke. I thank God that my mother isn't like that! I just couldn't stand that, because the kids end up just miserable. It's awful.

I started taking voice lessons about the time I was nine years old. I also took piano lessons from Cecelia Brauer and I studied for a few years with her in Merrick. Before that, I studied with Morton Estrin — who is excellent, and he is a real perfectionist. He also taught Billy Joel, and he is in Hicksville, Long Island. I studied with Cecelia Brauer for a few years, and then I went back to Morton Estrin again.

I also took lessons from Florence Hargrove on Long Island, then Terry Ariggio and a guy named Louis Polanski in New York City. Now I am studying with Guen Omeron, who I'm really happy with now. There is no such thing as a good teacher or a bad teacher. It's all chemistry and how you relate to a teacher. Their personality is as important as what they can teach you. Not only their personality, but how they explain things is very important. For a long time I didn't quite grasp the concept of how to breathe properly while singing.

Every voice teacher says, "Sing from your diaphram. Breath this way." I was told it again and again, but I never fully understood it, until I went to Guen. The way she described things made it suddenly all come clear. During the first lesson she pulled out an anatomy book, because you have to know where everything is, and what is going on while you're singing. That helped me a lot. We work with weights. You actually hold weights while you sing and do exercises, because your diaphram is a muscle, and that's how your voice gets stronger. It's not your voice — it's your muscles that give you the ability to sustain notes, and increase your range.

Guen has helped me a great deal with that. She was actually an opera singer, so she knows what it's like to be on the road, and she's had all of those experiences in her life, and she really knows what she's doing.

I started singing at the Metropolitan

Opera in New York City in the Children's Chorus, when I was about nine years old, and in fifth grade. I sang there in the fifth grade through eighth grade. That was an incredible, incredible experience. First of all, I love foreign languages. The Met is probably responsible for the start of my love of foreign languages. We'd have to know what we were singing, and we had the translations written on the score under everything that we were singing. It was very professional, and very strict, but really great. I was always very serious about it. I mean, community theater is fun and really great, but at the same time, I wanted to do something truly professional.

The teacher for the Children's Chorus at the Met, Mrs. Honer, would tell us, "Don't go down and bother the stars before the opera." I had a friend there whose name is Jennifer Hines, and naturally we used to sneak down and knock on the opera stars' doors! We used to walk right in their dressing rooms! We even knocked on Placido Domingo's door! They were always so nice to us, and so willing to answer any questions, and take pictures and things. We used to do it all the time. I got to meet Renata Scotto, and Theresa Stratas, and Placido Domingo, and all these great opera singers. It was incredible just walking around that place, because you'd be walking down the hall and you'd see Luciano Pavarotti. When I did *La Boheme,* Placido Domingo was in the same production, and I worked with all of these fantastic people! I was just in the children's chorus, but it was an incredible experience just to be on stage with those people, and to work with Franco Zefferelli, and all these incredible directors. I worked with some really top notch people, and it was amazing. Obviously, it was something that other fifth graders couldn't really relate to at the time. That may have been a difference in my career outlook and my determination. I still went to the local birthday parties, and I was still in the school chorus, but at the same time, I was doing these other things.

It was also about the time when I was nine or ten, that I started going to professional auditions for television commercials and for theater in New York City. I would read *Show Business* magazine, and *Back Stage* and *Variety,* and circle the auditions that I was qualified for. And, my parents would figure out their work schedules so that they could take me, or my grandfather would take me in by train. I went on a million auditions before I ever landed anything. That's the thing about this business, you can go to auditions for two years, and not land a single role. But, I never got discouraged. I simply thought of every audition as experience, and I just kept at it and kept going. I even enjoyed the auditions themselves, because I just looked at them as an opportunity to sing. Also, my opinion was always, "Well, if I'm not right for this project, at least the director heard me sing, and maybe I'll get called for something else."

I always thought very optimistically, and I was never in the frame of mind that thought, "Oh, gee — they rejected me!" You have to deal with that a lot in this business, I'll tell you! I'm real used to that. That's why I don't take any of my success for granted. I know how much time and energy went into it, and the people close to me know too.

The first professional show that I did was *A Christmas Carol,* Sheldon Harnick and Michel LeGrand's version of it. That was also an incredible experience. It was done in Connecticut, and through that production, I ended up with my Equity card for the theater union. I was eleven at the time. That was really exciting, because I'd read all of those auditions that said, "Equity Members Only," and because I wasn't a member, I couldn't audition. And then I got a non-union commercial when I was twelve, for Key Bank. It was a commercial for this bank in upstate New York, and after that I started doing more TV commercials. Eventually, I got my Screen Actor's Guild card too. I did several TV commercials for a while, including one for Wendy's Hamburgers.

It was when I was twelve years old that I started writing songs, and recording my own demos. I got my four track recorder at that time. What was happening was that all of this commercial work was suddenly taking my time away from music, and I knew that I wasn't going to make a career out of TV commercials. The commercials were fun to do, but I knew that I really wanted to put all of my time and effort into my music.

That was always what was on my mind — thinking of my music in long range terms. You can make a lot of money by doing commercials, and it's tempting to just give up on the singing and stay in commercials. But I knew that what I really wanted to do was to pursue music. So, I gave up my commercial career when I was about fifteen.

When I was twelve years old I had an English teacher named Dr. Deck. He was one of my all-time favorite teachers. One day he came into our classroom, and said to me, "Did you hear about this?" And, he was carrying a piece of paper announcing a songwriting contest that a local radio station was running. By some odd coincidence, that same day, my dad had written down the information about the contest. Everyone knew that this would be something that I would be interested in. So, I entered this songwriting contest where you had to write a song about America. I was twelve years old, and the contest was for people twenty-two years old and under. And, there was another category for twenty-three and over. In the "twenty-two and under" category I won the first place prize, which was a thousand dollars!

I used to put all of my money in the bank. At that time, I was always saving my money for college. In the long range, the thousand dollars I won in the contest ended up being used for my recording studio. The radio station, WOR, played my song, and announced that I had won, which was really exciting. The song that I wrote was called "I Come From America."

"I Come From America" was based on personal experience. My dad has always worked for an airline, so we've always had the

I finally got to meet my hero — Billy Joel — at the Grammy Awards in 1988.

opportunity to travel a lot in the United States. We took a vacation every year, so the lyrics were like, "I did the hula in Hawaii, I went swimming in Peoria, Although I may visit Spain and Portugal, I come from America." It was based on places that I'd been, and then there were verses about how people from all different countries live in America. It was a cute little reggae-sounding song that I wrote on a synthesizer. The synthesizer was a cute little Casio keyboard that I asked for when I made my Confirmation at church — instead of asking for jewelry. When I got that, that's when I wrote that song. It was the type of machine where you could put the little drum beat on the song.

As I mentioned, the first song that I ever wrote was called "Make Sure You Know Your Classroom." I don't know what inspired me to do that. I don't know if I had some deep, hidden insecurity about starting school or what. I didn't think I did, but the words to the song were: "Make sure you know your classroom, Make sure you know your seat, I hope you find your teacher, I hope she looks so sweet. Make sure you know your classroom, Make sure you know your seat, I hope you find your teacher, Or you'll have to wait in the street." I couldn't even write at the time — I didn't even know how to physically write — because I hadn't even started school yet, so my sisters helped me write it out, and they helped me write out the notes on a big piece of staff paper. Obviously the song wasn't much, but maybe someday I'll do a re-mix of it! As silly as the song was, that was the beginning of my writing career.

Obviously, I didn't know what I was doing at that age, but it showed that someday I was going to eventually write music. From that point on, I'd write on and off. I remember writing a song when I was eight, called "My Puppy Grew." It was about my dog, Sam. Then I wrote a song when we went to New Jersey to visit my relatives, called "Lovely Day On The Farm." On another occasion I wrote a song called "Two Way Traffic Ahead," just because I wrote it in the car, and I saw a sign that said "Two Way Traffic Ahead." I used to write these little songs all of the time. They were really stupid songs, but obviously they were learning experiences.

My parents realized that they were silly little songs, but they figured, "She's only eight years old, let's at least encourage her to be creative. They'd tell me, "That's great . . . that's great!!!" So, I just kept going with my songwriting. Eventually, I wrote a song called "So Sweet The Music." I knew that my first songs were really silly, but "So Sweet The Music" was what I considered my first real composition and was of the calibre of what I was listening to on the radio at the time. It was kind of like an "I'd Like To Teach The World To Sing" type of song.

I wrote "Only In My Dreams" when I was thirteen. That was my first attempt at writing a pop-sounding song. A lot of people that I would sing it for would say, "How are you writing love songs? You're only thirteen years old!" I don't know. I was just kind of guessing and going by what I heard, and observing my older sisters, and taking ideas from movies that I had seen, and TV shows. It was my impression of what love was like. I couldn't even relate to my own songs until I was sixteen! Songs that I had written a few years before, I couldn't even relate to them. Some of my songs I haven't been able to relate to until this year!

The love songs that I wrote when I was thirteen and fourteen sounded like things that I heard about as far as subject matter, because I didn't know about falling in love. As far as melody and the beat goes, I've always loved Top 40 radio, and I based my music on what I heard over the airwaves. A lot of people put down pop songs, but you know when you hear a good pop song, you just can't get it out of your head for weeks. I love that element of a good pop song. No matter how much you analyze it, or put it down, people still enjoy pop songs.

The first records that I bought were very important to me. The first single that I remember getting was Elton John's "Crocodile

In "La Boheme" at the Met.

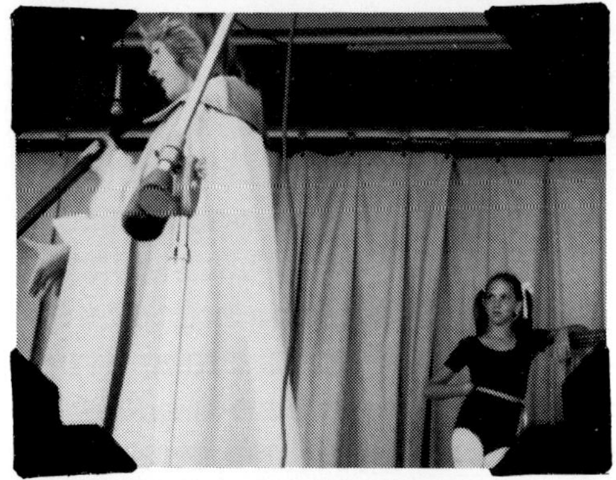

In "Cinderella," as the fairy Godmother's helper.

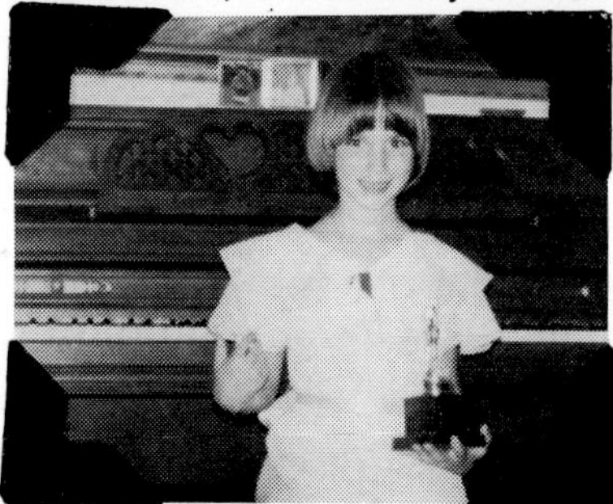

With my prize that I won at the age of six for playing the classical piano, at the CYO talent contest.

Ta Dah!

Debbie and Denise in "South Pacific" at Hofstra University.

Karen, Debbie, and Michele at the Town of Hempstead talent contest. We sang "Matchmaker" from "Fiddler On The Roof" and we took third place!

In 1978 at eight, in "South Pacific" at Sacred Heart Church.

As Baby Jane in "Gypsy" in 1982.

Rock." It was released when I was really, really little, but I heard it later on, and I really wanted a copy of it. I still have my copy of that single, with my name printed on it, in pencil. The first album that I remember asking for was Billy Joel's "52nd Street," and I received a copy of it for Christmas. I was so excited about that album when I got it, and I played it constantly and learned all of the words to it, and I sang along with it.

Of course, after that, the next time that Billy Joel came to town to appear in concert, I had to go. Before that, the only concerts that I had seen were The Beach Boys, and — before any other concert — I had seen Liberace! I loved Liberace. My mom was thinking, "What's with this seven-year-old kid asking for Liberace tickets?!" My grandparents took me to see him. I loved entertainers, and I loved the fact that Liberace was such a showman. During the concert, in the actual piano playing, I could actually hear mistakes that he made, because I had learned to play some of those same pieces — like Chopin's "Minute Waltz." I can still remember him playing that. But it didn't matter if he missed a note or two, because his showmanship was so great, and the audience didn't notice the musical errors he made.

When I heard the music on Billy Joel's "52nd Street" album, to me — that was rock and roll! The whole feeling of Billy's concert was amazing. I danced through the whole show. My whole family went to that concert. My dad got there early when the tickets went on sale, in fact he was the first person in line at Nassau Coliseum to buy tickets. Somehow, we ended up with tickets in the sky — in the upper section of the coliseum — I think it was because of scalpers purchasing all of the front section tickets or something. We sat far away from the stage, but I didn't care. I remember that concert, and dancing through the whole thing. I remember exactly where we sat, and everything. I can still picture it.

Billy Joel's music meant a lot to me, especially because he also played the piano and wrote his own songs. I just loved his piano playing, and I loved his melodies. Anyone who is a fan of Billy Joel just loves his lyrics. At the time I couldn't really relate to songs like "Honesty" and "Zanzibar." I especially loved his real rock and roll songs, like "My Life" and "Big Shot." I always loved the sound of rock and roll. Anyone can get into a beat, no matter how old they are, or where they're from.

At the time, I never really thought, "I'd like to meet Billy Joel and sing with him." I knew that I wanted to do what Billy Joel was doing, but meeting him didn't cross my mind at the time.

When I was twelve years old, I appeared in my first movie. I was an "extra" in the movie *Ghostbusters.* It's hard to believe that that movie was shot that long ago! At the time I was doing commercials, and I was called to appear in *Ghostbusters.* I remember hearing that title for the first time — it sounded so weird! I kept thinking of "Dustbusters" every time I heard "Ghostbusters." Before everyone had heard of it, I'd think, "Ghostbusters?" It sounds really bizarre!

I remember the scene I appeared in. It was filmed at a restaurant in New York City called Tavern On The Green. When you watch the movie closely, and you don't blink, in the restaurant scene, there's a table with balloons, and there's a girl with a pink bow in her hair, supposedly having her birthday party — that's me!

That was a scene with Harold Ramis, and I remember shooting that scene over and over again. What I remember the most was the fact that the scene was shot between ten o'clock at night and five o'clock in the morning, and it was freezing cold. It was shot in the winter, and the doors were open for the lighting cables and the electrical equipment. In the scene, they kept putting food down on the table, but we weren't allowed to eat any of it until the last "take," because they had to keep using the same food over and over again. Since I was supposed to be the birthday girl, they kept bringing this chocolate cake and setting it down in front of us, and we kept going for about ten hours without eating any of it. You couldn't believe when the director said, "It's a wrap," and the scene was finished, that cake was in a million pieces! It was destroyed almost immediately! Everyone kept grabbing squares and slices and handsful out of it.

When the film was released, I remember going to see it on the first night at the Holiday Park movie theater in Merrick. I remember screaming at the screen: "There I am! THERE I AM!!!" I swear, you only see me for about one second, and there is this waiter standing in front of me half of the time. I was also an extra in a couple of movies that I never did see, like *Sweet Liberty* and *The Book of Daniel* and *Manhattan Project.* All of those experiences were really fun. A lot of kids wouldn't think of it as fun, because shooting those scenes take a lot of long hours. It's a lot of "hurry up" and "wait" involved in movie making. There's more "waiting" to shoot a scene, than there is actual on-camera work.

You get to know a lot of the same kids from doing commercials, and doing "extra" work on films. I got to meet a lot of people, and I kind of hung out with the other kids on the set, between "takes."

I sang at a place called Something Different in Manhattan, when I was twelve, thirteen, fourteen, and fifteen years old. I performed songs that I wrote there. It was a little ice cream parlor. It was like a dessert nightclub for kids. A lot of people who sang there went on to big things: Scott Grimes, who is an actor and now has a solo album; Ricki Lake, who was in the movie *Hairspray*; and a lot of kids who are in the business. I used to love going there. All I got paid for it was an ice cream sundae at the end of the night. All of us kids loved to sing for our dessert there, because they had the best desserts in the city! It was also a great place to showcase.

I sang the songs that I wrote, and I did a Billy Joel medley there, and I played harmonica and the piano in the middle of it. I used to sing two songs there. Everyone sang two songs. This would be at four o'clock in the afternoon, on Sundays.

When i performed at Something Different, I remember that kids used to lie about their age. I never had to, or wanted to, do that. Every year the kids would have a birthday, and they'd still be the same age they were a year ago! The only reason that I would think of doing that was because, if I'm eighteen, and I'd say I was fifteen, people would think that I'm really good for a fifteen-year-old. But that's not the right attitude to have. You should want to be really good, no matter what age you are.

The only time that I ever lied about my age, was when I was fifteen, and I was at the audition for *Les Miserables.* For the role I tried out for, Eponine, they wanted a "legal eighteen-year-old," and they didn't know my age. The producers were interested in me until they asked my agent my age, and then it was all over. But, I did get called back three times for that role. I would really still like to perform that role someday. I know that there is going to be a movie version of that, and I'd love to play Eponine in it!

I'll never forget going to one of the "call backs" of *Les Miserables.* First, our car broke down on the way. Then we got into a cab, and the cab driver couldn't speak English. Then, we were going over the 59th Street Bridge, and there was a fire on the bridge — in a car. It was like: "Over the river and through the woods" to get to this call-back. I finally got there, and it was like, "You'll never believe what happened to me on the way here . . ." It was so ridiculous it was funny!

All of these experiences, the commercials, the "extra" roles in the movies, and the piano and voice lessons, made me want to pursue a career in the entertainment business even more. I love performing, no matter what it is — acting, singing, or playing the piano — anything that gives me a chance to perform!

I love to entertain . . . just give me a microphone and a rug! This was taken in Brooklyn at a street fair

Singing for my ice cream at Something Different (right).

Merokian a finalist for 'Annie'

Deborah Gibson, age 10, of Merrick is one of the 10 finalists for the national tour of "Annie." The tour is scheduled to begin

Debbie Gibson

rehearsal on August 17 and will travel all over the country for six months to a year.

Now four feet seven inches tall, Deborah is the maximum height allowed for the part. She is the daughter of Joseph and Diane, and this is her last opportunity to get the part before she "outgrows" the role.

"We're sitting on eggs," sa r. Gibson, who expects th

Deborah will be notified within the next few weeks.

Not idle, Deborah has a role in "Annie, Get Your Gun" to be presented at Eisenhower Park on July 17 and 18. She is busy rehearsing four hours a day.

The Gibsons have three other daughters; Karen, 15; Michele 14; and Denise, 6; all of wh play the piano and sing.

MERRICK, N.Y. 11566 THURSDAY, MAY 26, 1977

Deborah Gibson

Piano virtuoso

A First Place award in the recent CYO talent contest was won by six-year-old Deborah Gibson. Deborah won her award in the Classical Piano Solo category. The talented youngster is in the First Grade at the Camp Avenue School. Her parents, Mr. and Mrs. Joseph Gibson of 1684 Sterling Avenue, are the parents of four daughters in all, three of hom took part in the contes borah has been playing th for only one year.

Among finalists

Deborah Gibson is among the finalists for a part in the Broadway play, "Annie", at the Alvin Theater. She has been selected from among 1,000 youngsters by the show's director, Martin Charin. She is the daughter of Mr. and Mrs. James Gibson.

Deborah has performed in many shows in the community and entertained at the Holly Patterson Senior Citizens Centre. For the past two summers she has been a member of the Town of Hempstead and Nassau Repertory roups performing in their sum- er theatrical productions.

Deborah Gibson

Merokians's song is super!

Deborah Gibson of Merrick, a 13-year-old eight grade student from Brookside Junior High School, was the first place winner in the statewide competition which was sponsored by the New York State Congress of Parents and Teachers.

Deborah's original song, "I

Deborah Gibson

Dream of America" was the first place winner in the Music Category. Her entry will now be entered in the National competition which will be judged in Chicago, and the winners will be announced at the national convention in the WOR Radio songwriters competition. She is currently appearing in New York City at "Something Different" and performs in the "Youngstars" show every Sunday, where she sings h[er] original music.

Youngster makes debut

Deborah Gibson

Deborah Gibson, daughter of Joseph and Diane Gibson of Merrick, will make her professional theatrical debut as Belinda in "A Christmas Carol" at the Hartman Theatre in Stamford, Connecticut December 10 through 26.

Deborah, a student at the Brookside Junior High School, is the granddaughter of Mr. and Mrs. Albert Pustizzi of Horace Court, Bellmore.

She has performed at the Metropolitan Opera in "La Boheme", "Hansel and Gretel", and "Le Rossignol", and also in "Gypsy", "The Sound of Music", "Annie Get Your Gun", and "South Pacific" for the Bellmore Jewish Center productions at Calhoun High School.

Recently, the 12 year old was in "The Book of Daniel" with Timothy Hutton. Deborah is also a pianist and writes and records music.

MEROKIANS ON STAGE: Joe Gibson and daughters Denise and Deborah of Merrick are appearing in the upcoming Gray Wig production of "South Pacific", which will be performed at John Cranford Adams Playhouse on the Hofstra South Campus. Performance dates are Friday and Saturday, September 2 and 3, at 8:30 p.m., Sunday, September 4, at 3 p.m., Friday and Saturday, September 9 and 10, at 8:30 p.m., and Sunday, September 11, at 7 p.m. Tickets are priced at $7.50 for all performances and $6.50 for senior citizens and students with special rates for groups of 25 or more. For further information, contact the box office (9 a.m. to 5 p.m.) [at] 560-6644.

4

Songwriter

Setting up my own recording studio in the garage of our house was a very important step towards achieving my goal of becoming a professional recording artist. Basically, what I had been doing up until that point was going into other recording studios to record demos of my songs.

At this point, my parents realized that I was very serious about writing and recording my own songs. This was when I was twelve years old. We all realized that I had a future in show business, and Mom and Dad did what they could to help me.

When I was twelve, I was writing songs *every day*! All of a sudden, I was just like writing non-stop. And, the songs were getting better, and better, and better. My parents realized this, and I realized this, and it was giving me a lot of pleasure.

On a typical day, I would come home from school, and I'd write a song. And I'd remember my mom coming in from work around five or six o'clock, and me saying, "Mom, Mom — listen to this new song I wrote!" And she'd say, "Can you wait a minute, so I can put down my pocketbook!" There were some times when she would listen to my new song, and say, "Oh, that's nice." And other times, she would say, "That was pretty good, you know." For a little while, it was like she was just humoring me, but she knew that I had creative potential, but she also knew that every song was not a hit. Throughout it all, she was very encouraging.

It got to the point where I said to her, "What am I supposed to do with these songs? I can go on just making piano and vocal demo tapes with my songs, or I can take them to the next step." So, I suggested, "Why don't I go to a studio, and see what I can do there?" Even before I started writing, I would go into the studio and make demo tapes, just of my singing. At this point I had already gotten a little taste of the studio. Since the time I was nine, I was making little demos of my singing. From the very start, I always liked being in the studio.

What happened is that I started going to other studios to demo my songs, and one of the guys at the studio would set up a drum machine for me and set up the keyboards, and he would put down parts. It was good, but it wasn't exactly what I wanted. So, I was looking at the control panel at the studio, and I thought, "I could learn what all of these little gadgets can do, and do this myself!"

My first professional quality tape recorder was a four-track machine, which you can't do too much on, but it was a good machine to start on. It really served its purpose, and it

Playing piano at home, while my dog, Sam, "lends me a paw" on the keyboard!

was great for putting ideas down. Just to explain the machine: a four-track recorder basically allows you to put down tracks one at a time. On one track you would make up a drum beat on a drum machine — and record it, and then while that drum beat's playing, you could record a bass line, and you'd have them both on separate tracks. Nowadays, records are made on twenty-four tracks, or forty-eight tracks. But, with a four-track, you can do what is known as "bounce down," which means you can say record drums on one track, bass on another, and a keyboard on another, and you can combine them all on the fourth track, and then you'd have three open tracks again. And, you keep doing that whenever you record a new part — whether it's percussion, a guitar, background vocals — or whatever. You can also alter the volume of any of the individual instruments. So, my little four-track machine was like a little portable studio for me.

For the drum parts, I got a drum machine — a synthesizer and a little reel-to-reel tape recorder, and my four-track, and that was basically it — my first recording studio. This was all set up in half of the garage. We had a two car garage, and the half of it that we had used as a TV room, was suddenly filled with my musical instruments and recording equipment. Unfortunately, we didn't soundproof the garage — much to my little sister's dismay — because, Denise's room was right above the garage!

Eventually, we upgraded to a twelve-track studio, which just meant that I could do more. I got more keyboards, and a better drum machine, and a sequencer, and lots of stuff. This was all set up just so I could record my demo tapes, and that was long before my recording contract or any of that.

When I recorded the demo for the song "Shake Your Love," I'll never forget Denise waking up for school the next morning and asking, "Was I dreaming, or were you recording a song called 'Shake Your Love?' Because I swear I've heard that phrase over and over again in my sleep!" Poor Denise put up with a lot.

Usually it was just me in the recording studio that we put together. I would just lock myself in the room. There were just keyboard and drum machines back then, so I'd do everything. I'd do a bass line on the keyboard, and play all of the parts, and then I got into using some live stuff on the demos. I'd call up Tommy Williams, and ask him to play the guitar, and then eventually I started working with the band. I would call Kirk Powers to play the bass, or have Adam Tese come in to do some sax, or whatever. We would do some overdubs, and other additional tracks on the songs that I had written and partially recorded. Eventually I got into doing that, which is basically producing, but its like working with other people. Just doing these demos gave me a lot of experience producing.

What happened is that my parents and I eventually approached an entertainment attorney who listened to my demos. At this point I had dozens of demos completed for him to listen to.

Basically, my mom and I had been banging on doors for quite some time. Let's say I'd go on an audition for a commercial, and I'd be in an office building, and I'd see the words 'Management Company" or "Music Management" painted on one of the doors, and I'd knock on the door. My mom and I were always very gutsy about knocking on doors without appointments. We figured that it couldn't hurt to ask. We'd be in the Fisk Building in New York City a lot, and that's where my publicist, David Salidor has his office. There are a lot of entertainment businesses based there — agents and managers and stuff. I always had my demo tapes with me, so we'd just knock on the doors, and I'd say, "Hi, my name is Deborah Gibson and I write songs and I have a demo I'd like you to hear. Here's my picture and resume, which I just happen to have with me!"

For a while, in the beginning of my career, I was represented by an entertainment lawyer. This lawyer had been recommended to me by my commercial agent at the time. Basically, he was just the friend of a friend, who was in the music business. It was this particular attorney who made the initial contact with Atlantic Records. Specifically, he contacted their dance music department. At this point I had several demos of songs that I felt really strongly about, most of which ended up on my first album. Our initial meeting with the attorney was not one of our "knocking on the door" impromptu meetings. He was impressed with what he heard on the demo tapes, and he lined up a meeting with Atlantic's dance department.

Before they decided to offer me a recording contract, the dance department at Atlantic must have listened to fifty of my demos. They just wanted to keep hearing things, to make sure that I had a follow-up song if they agreed to release a twelve-inch single of "Only In My Dreams." They wanted to make sure that the song wasn't just a fluke. They were thinking, "What if she just wrote one cute song, and that's it?"

Well, I proved myself to them, but only to get myself signed to a "twelve-inch" deal and not an album deal. Atlantic's only obligation was that they would release "Only In My Dreams" as a twelve-inch dance single for clubs, and then see how it did. That was fine with me at the time, because that was my big chance to have a record of any sort released, and I would have something to promote. It gave me a way to show people what I could really do, which was the whole point. Atlantic said that based on how the twelve-inch did, they'd release a seven-inch single to the radio stations. And based on how the single did, they'd release an album.

When the twelve-inch single was released, the whole family sprang into action. We had our whole family support system, and all of our friends ready to go. They would call the radio stations to request the song, and they would go into the dance clubs and ask the DJ to play my record. They'd also bring copies of the record into the clubs, and get them to play it. Sometimes my friends would beat the record promoters into the clubs with copies of "Only In My Dreams!" We had recorded the song at the end of 1986, and it was released in the beginning of 1987.

I remember that winter, a friend of mine went on a vacation in Florida, and she took a copy of the record with her. While she was there, she took it to the clubs, and they played it, and the record got a great response. Then the Atlantic Records promotion people went into the same clubs, and said, "Here is this new record, 'Only In My Dreams,' " and the D.J.s said, "Oh, we have that already — one of Debbie's friends brought it in!"

To me, "Only In My Dreams" was always more of a "pop" record than a "dance" record. It had a good beat and everything, but it still was a very listenable song. It wasn't strictly a dance record, so I had a lot of confidence in it. Eventually Atlantic released a seven-inch single to radio stations, and when that happened, our family really went wild.

Everyone who heard "Only In My Dreams" only on the radio, thought that the song just came out in the summer of 1987, but it actually came out in January. It took eight months before it peaked on the pop charts. It was a long climb. It was like on the dance charts for thirty-three weeks! It ended up being the biggest selling twelve-inch single of the year! It only made it to number twelve on the "Club Play" chart, but ended up peaking at Number Four on the Pop Chart. It became a bigger pop hit than a dance hit.

When the single was released to the radio stations, everyone we knew called the radio stations and requested the song. Based on the response that the record received on the request lines, the radio stations realized that it was going to be a huge hit, and they began playing it more, and it was added to playlists all across the country.

At the time, I was busy doing "track dates" at dance clubs around the country. That's where you sing your song to prerecorded tracks. You sing live, but the instrumentals and the background vocals are on tape. I must have done about a hundred club appearances to promote "Only In My Dreams." This went on from January to August of 1987. This had me on a really intense schedule. I knew that all I needed to do was to promote myself, to get my music heard, before I had an audience all my own. So, I went crazy — doing every interview, every personal appearance, and everything that I could.

Performing at the Limelight in New York City was the debut club date that I did with "Only In My Dreams." Not long after that I performed at another club in New York City called 1018. My schedule would call for me to do a club performance at ten o'clock, and another one at midnight, and another one at two in the morning! I would get on a plane at seven in the morning, I would go to the next city, and I would go to the radio stations during the day, I would give interviews until late afternoon, and then I would do the track dates at night. I did that all summer long in 1987. I was also doing that when I was in school, doing all of my traveling on the weekends. I would go to school Monday through Friday, or sometimes Monday through Thursday, or sometimes Tuesday through Friday. And, I'd be doing all of my promotion work on the weekends. No one I went to school with had any idea how hard I was working. A lot of the kids in school were thinking, "Oh, she's lucky to have all of those extra days off from school." Well, let me tell you, it was a lot of work! They didn't have any idea how I spent my weekends. But, that's what I wanted to do.

I still made time for the regular things. My booking agent was probably the only booking agent who had times marked in a client's performing calendar that read: "Three days off for High School Prom." And, I had to make sure that I did that, or else I would have ended up working that weekend, and one day regretting it. Events like your high school prom are things that everyone has to do once, and you don't want to miss it!

After the single version of "Only In My Dreams" became a hit, Atlantic Records was going, "O.K., the single's really hot — where's the album!?" So, we only had about six weeks to come up with the rest of the album! Because we needed to come up with the rest of the album so quickly, the recording was done in several different locations, depending upon studio booking times, and everyone's schedule.

I had six weeks to record the whole album, and we had production going on in Florida, in Brooklyn, and in Manhattan. I was jumping around, flying all over the countryside, because I wanted to be a creative part of all of the tracks. While all of this was going on, I was still doing the "track dates' on the weekends!

Lewis Martineé was working on the song "Play The Field" at International Sound studios in Miami. John Morales and Sergio Munzibai were working on "Between The Lines" and "Red Hot" at Quad Recording studios in Manhattan. Fred Zarr was working in Brooklyn at Z studios and I was working on the songs in Brooklyn that I was producing and co-producing myself. I wanted to be there for everything, and I was flying all over the place. I ended up with a terrible case of laryngitis because I was so run down.

My whole first album was basically recorded while I had laryngitis. I'm used to performing under pressure, and in the theater you learn that "the show must go on." So, the engineer in the studio would hit the "Play and Record" buttons on the console, and somehow I would sing. As soon as we were done with the recordings, I would have no voice left at all! It was a pretty crazy time!

The album came out, but it took a while for the album to get going on the charts. It moved at a very slow and steady pace, but after two years, it sold over three million copies! My first album, "Out Of The Blue," was released in August 1987. The video for "Only In My Dreams" we shot in June of that year, just as the single was getting ready to enter the Top 40 charts.

The plot of my first video was kind of a mystery to me. Basically I just followed the director. I still don't quite know what the concept is for that video, because I didn't have a lot of creative control over the filming of it. The idea of putting the carousel scene in the video was mine, and to me, that's what made the video very "me." That was the "fun" element of the video, and it made sense to interject that into it. To me, it made the video seem like a fun, summery, amusement park kind of a video. To me that made sense, because while I was filming the rest of the video, I was saying things to the director like, "Excuse me, what is this bed doing on the beach?" and "Why is this lady hanging clothes up, and waving 'goodbye' to me?" and "Why is this classroom on the beach?" To me, it was quite funny.

The record company was paying for the video, so I just said O.K. to the plot of the video, but I didn't compromise myself to the point of doing something in it that I didn't want to do. I figured, "It's totally harmless, I may as well just go along with this. It doesn't matter." The sequence of running on the beach was one of my ideas. It seems funny to say, but, "I have no idea what that video is all about!"

At the time, everybody involved in the video had their own idea of what they wanted me to look like, and who they wanted me to be. I think that I stayed pretty true to myself through it all. A lot of people said, "Put her in something black." And I kept saying, "That's not me at all." The thing is that every girl singer you see on MTV, comes out looking sexy, and dressed in black. I didn't want to do that and end up looking like everybody else. I wanted to go out of my way to avoid that. Things like that I insisted on.

In the "Only In My Dreams" video, I was wearing this cute kind of sailor dress, and some people thought that was a little bit too cutesy. But, that's me. I have to admit, I love "fun" and "cute." I'm very comfortable in that sort of an outfit. I don't think that you have to dress in an out-and-out sexy fashion to sell records. In that video, I didn't have my black hat on because I had a different haircut and a hat wouldn't have worked. My hair was layered on top.

It was also my idea from the very beginning to be accompanied during all of my "track date" appearances by two male dancers. Buddy Casimano was with me from the very beginning. How this all came about, is that when I was starting out with Atlantic Records, I had a commercial agency that represented me called F.B.I. (Frontier Booking, Inc.), and Buddy went to my high school with me. He had wanted to get involved in making commercials, and he was a year older than me. The only thing I knew about him was that he was a really good dancer. We had a talent contest in school, and both Buddy and I entered the contest. Once I saw him, I thought, "Wow! He's great." He is not only a great dancer, but he is a great gymnast, and he does these incredible backflips and things. That's what he did in the talent show, and when I saw him in action, I knew that he had won the contest. It turned out, however, that the football team won first prize by singing a rap song, called "The Calhoun Colt Shuffle"; Buddy and his dance partner, Linda, came in second, and I didn't win anything — because there was no third prize.

In the contest I sang a song that I wrote called "Somebody Loves You." The funny thing was that Buddy was certain that I was going to win first prize, and I was positive that he was going to win first prize — and neither of us did!

At the time, I didn't know Buddy at all. Meanwhile, he just happens to walk into my commercial agency, and he sees my picture on the wall. So just to make conversation, he says, "Oh, that girl goes to my high school." At that point, my first single hadn't been released yet. So, Scott at F.B.I. says to Buddy, "I think that she's looking for dancers. You're a dancer, right?" And Buddy goes, "Yeah!"

So, I get home from school one afternoon, and there is a message on my answering machine that said, "Hi, Debbie." (Since my close friends all call me "Deborah," that was the first and last time that he ever called me "Debbie!") Anyway, the message goes on: "This is Buddy Casimano. You don't know me. I go to your school, and I'm a year older than you. Scott at F.B.I. mentioned to me that you might be looking for some dancers, so give me a call. My number is . . ."

I gave him a call. I knew that he was an incredible dancer, and we just talked to him, and my family and I liked his personality and his attitude, and we hired him. Then we were looking for another dancer, and we went through a lot of dancers. It was hard to find someone who was going to be dedicated, who had a good attitude, and who was a good dancer. It was a rare combination really. We went through a lot of dancers, who worked with Buddy and me, and we eventually found Keith Stewart, who has been with me for a long time now.

The reason that I had the dancers in my act was that I wanted to do more on stage than the average performer. Obviously, you don't get paid that much to do track dates, and it meant less money for me, but my attitude has always been: "I don't care if I don't make a cent — I just want to put on a good show!" And, that's my honest attitude. A lot of people would look at me and say, "Oh, right! I'm sure." But that is my attitude to this day. That is all I want to do. I can go crazy on the production elements of my shows: "I want fireworks! I want this . . . and that!" Whatever it takes to complement the show.

I don't want my production to upstage me, but I put on a strong show to begin with, and if you highlight that with a good production, then that's it — you'll blow people away — and that's what I want to do! Even with the little club dates that we were doing to tracks in the beginning, I wanted a "show" element to my act, and the dancers added the right visual element.

I would never lip sync, I always sang

"live" to the background tapes. That can be a little boring, just watching one person singing on stage for a half hour, and choreography doesn't look right if you don't do it with a couple of people. Performing with two male dancers just seemed to work out perfectly. Even back then, I felt that my "track dates" were all very entertaining shows. I always want to be the best at whatever I'm doing, and I decided that "I want to have the best 'track act' show possible."

We found Keith through an audition that we had held. My sister Karen ran the auditions for me, and Keith had just come to the audition to accompany someone else. Up until that time, I had another dancer who performed with Buddy, but he didn't work out. Well, it was Karen who convinced Keith to audition. He wasn't even going to try out. Well, all you have to do is ask Keith something once, and he's like: "O.K.!" Keith also teaches dance, and the guy that he accompanied to the audition was one of his students.

At the audition, my sister found out that Keith could not only dance, but that he was also an incredible singer. I have already written a song for him, and I want to produce and record him eventually. I feel that he's a star waiting to happen. I love him, and I think that he is great. I'm like his biggest fan. He writes songs and he is involved in Showstoppers National Dance Competitions. Keith's first show with me was at Magic Mountain, an amusement park in California, in 1988.

I'm glad that I've got friends like Keith (left) and Buddy (right) with me when I'm on tour. We have a great time on stage together!

With Julie Brown on "Club MTV."

5

Out of the Blue

The release of my first album, "Out Of The Blue," was really exciting for me. Since I wrote all of the songs on it, I had literally been working on it for years. The first thing we had to do when we put the album together was to figure out which songs of mine we wanted to include on it.

There were some pretty obvious choices for me. My concept of what an album should be like is that every song should be strong enough to be a hit single. I don't like an album to have a weak link on it. I think that's what makes a really good album. That's what made Madonna's "True Blue" album so great, and made Billy Joel's "52nd Street" great. I don't like albums where there are three good songs on it, and the rest of it is horrid.

So, on both of my albums, I thought of every song as a potential hit single. I just wanted every song to be strong, and in my mind it was pretty obvious what had a good hook, and on the first album, I was really looking for songs of mine that had a real dance/pop feeling to them. The dance clubs were so good to me with my first single, I wanted to make sure that there was enough danceable material on the album. I also included the two ballads on the album as well. I wanted the tone of the album to be real upbeat and fun.

To explain the songs that are included on my first album, here is a cut-by-cut rundown of all ten songs:

"OUT OF THE BLUE"

I got the idea for "Out Of The Blue," through this guy I went out with, who was visiting our school. I hadn't seen him since elementary school, and he suddenly came to see the kids he used to know at our school. So, it happened "out of the blue."

When I write my songs, it's not like one song is about one experience only, but an individual experience which might trigger an idea. That's what happened with this song.

"STAYING TOGETHER"

"Staying Together" I remember writing in Florida, in a hotel room. I was doing "track dates," and I got a melody in my head that I had to write down immediately. After my mom and I went to bed, I got up in the middle of the night, turned on the bathroom light, and wrote the whole thing right then.

To me, it's just a funky, fun kind of song, with a little attitude to it. Mom and Karen were both asleep, and I turned on the bathroom light, and wrote it in the hallway that led to the bathroom. I was lying on the floor in the hall with the door to the bathroom

With my "Double Platinum" award for "Out Of The Blue," which I received on my eighteenth birthday. You can see the candles of my cake behind the albums.

opened just a crack, so that I didn't wake up Mom and Karen.

It's still one of my favorite songs. It's funny, but it's my worst charting record, in terms of sales and popularity, but I don't care, because its one of my favorites. I love performing this song "live" in concert, because I love the energy of it.

"ONLY IN MY DREAMS"

"Only In My Dreams" was just a phrase that I made up a story around. I didn't realize the impact that that particular song would have. To some people it was just a cute little pop song, but I got a lot of letters from people who were really touched by it. I heard from several people who were really sick, or depressed, or having some hardship in their family, but, after they heard this song, they felt that they had the courage to carry on pursuing their dreams.

Some people wrote to me and said, "You helped me to realize that I could pull through, because I have dreams too." I didn't realize that it would affect people that way. It proved to be very inspirational to some people, and that was really touching to me. In fact, I recently heard that a child came out of a coma while listening to "Out Of The Blue." When I hear stories like that, it just makes me want to cry. Writing songs is just something that I do, that I don't really think about, and I don't realize that they can affect people, and touch their lives like that. It makes up for all of those people who turn up their noses at pop songs!

"Only In My Dreams" was my first real attempt at writing a pop kind of song. It was the first time that I got my drum machine going with a really funky beat!

"FOOLISH BEAT"

"Foolish Beat" I wrote coming home on an airplane. You know how you get in that pensive mood when you're on airplanes? To me "Foolish Beat" sounds like a song that you would write on an airplane.

That was the first song that I produced by myself, in a major recording studio. And, that song was also my first Number One hit, so it has a lot of meaning to it. I knew exactly how I wanted it to sound right from the start.

The song itself is based on no particular experience whatsoever, because I wrote it when I was fourteen years old. What kind of traumatic romance could I have gone through at fourteen? Still, a love song like that, anyone could relate to. Whether you're thirteen, and it's like: "I'm in love with this kid, and he doesn't love me, and my life is over!" or you're forty years old and your marriage has gone wrong. To me, you can relate to it on any level that you want to. It's like that with any love song.

"RED HOT"

"Red Hot" I wrote in Florida, and it's probably my "danciest" song, because Florida has such a strong dance base. New York and Florida are the two places where my first record broke — in the dance clubs. So, I wrote that in Florida, as kind of a fun and upbeat song.

I'm thinking about doing that song in concert this fall, because it always gets the crowd going.

"WAKE UP TO LOVE"

"Wake Up To Love" I wrote in social studies class. I was falling asleep in class one day, and I said to myself, "wake up!" And, I started thinking, "wake up to love!" and developed a story around it.

That song's about when you have someone really close in your life, and it's like, "You stupid fool, would you just wake up and see we're in love already!"

New Year's Eve 1987 at 4-D in New York City (left). At an in-store autograph signing, with one of my youngest fans (right).

"SHAKE YOUR LOVE"

"Shake Your Love" is the same thing. It's basically about someone you just can't get off of your mind. I also wrote it when I was fourteen or fifteen. This is the song that I woke my sister Denise up with when I was recording the demo, in our garage, underneath her bedroom.

"FALLEN ANGEL"

I don't even remember where I was when I wrote "Fallen Angel." It's a song about the good guys and the bad guys. Like a "boy from the wrong side of the tracks" kind of a thing. The ending, when the music drops out and the voices continue, was one of Fred Zarr's ideas.

I would demo the songs, and we would get all of the ideas basically from that, so that the finished product would sound like what I originally envisioned. But, that ending was Fred's idea. It sounds like a sort of tribal dance at the end. I think it's cool!

I used to do three songs when I did "track dates." I used to do all extended versions of "Fallen Angel," "Shake Your Love," and "Only In My Dreams." I would do about an eight minute version of each song!

"PLAY THE FIELD"

"Play the Field" was just an expression that my mom always used. When Karen was in high school, she dated the same guy from tenth grade until her second year in college. My mom would say to her, "You're too young to be so serious. You have to play the field." That's where I got the idea from for that song.

That is my attitude, too. I like to date. I don't really want to be tied down at this point. After all, I'm still just a teenager!

"BETWEEN THE LINES"

"Between The Lines," hey — that's the title of this book! I wrote that song with this book in mind!

No, actually it's funny how I got the idea for this song. I was staring at my notebook, and I really wanted to write a song, and I couldn't think of anything, and I didn't have any ideas. So, I looked at the piece of paper long enough until I saw nothing but lines. And then the title came to me: "Between The Lines." After that I just developed the story about how you can just pick up vibes from someone, you read between the lines.

When it finally comes time to record an album, the most important people involved are your producers and/or co-producers. One of the best people I have ever worked with is Fred Zarr. The same attorney who took me to Atlantic Records introduced me to Fred. Fred had done a lot of arranging and a lot of keyboard playing and session work. He had worked with Madonna, and with Village People, and a lot of different recording artists.

My first album was like a "first" for him as a producer. Although he had been responsible for a lot of the records that he arranged, he just didn't get the proper credit. Like he always said, he just chalked it up to "experience." He hadn't been credited as a full-fledged producer, but on my album he was.

It took a while for Fred and I to get used to working with each other in the beginning. I was very headstrong, and I didn't want to trust anyone I didn't know — with my music. Also, I had a lot of proving to do myself, too. A lot of people had the attitude: "Who is this little sixteen-year-old girl, coming in and telling us what to do?"

The chemistry between Fred and I definitely worked though. The songs came out still sounding very much like my songs. It kept my whole "feel," but, Fred adds a nice edge to my music, that I don't quite have yet. He

suggested several things that ended up working nicely.

We totally compromise, and come up with ideas together. I'll cite an example. When we were recording the song "Only In My Dreams," on the part where I sing the line "can't remember when I felt good, baby," Fred suggested the "felt good," and then I said, "baby." We totally work together like that!

On songs like that, we definitely really clicked. Fred is my other set of ears. He is the only other person I trust at this point, as far as producing my songs. He is excellent. Hurray for Fred!

When an album is released, there are a lot of promotional appearances and things that people don't realize that you do, because you do them on a small level. You may only be reaching twenty people at a time, or fifty people at a time, or one hundred people at a time, but it all adds up and helps you to create a base audience. That is a really important aspect of promotion. It's also really important for you to go to radio stations, and to meet these guys who play your records, and to show them that you really appreciate it. I *do* appreciate it — obviously. People wouldn't hear my music if it wasn't for radio. It's like, you have to give back something. I think that it has a different effect, once you've met a D.J. or a program director in person. They feel like they're not just playing a stranger's record. They know who they're listening to, and I know who they are when it's concert night, and the concert is being sponsored by this or that radio station. Once I meet the people at the radio station, I can say, "I know them — they're the first people to play my record in this part of the country!" That way, it makes the whole job of promotion much more personal.

In the beginning, I did all sorts of promotional events and concerts: anything that allowed me to get out and play in front of people — even if it was to tracks. I remember doing a radio promotional show in Florida where I opened for The Monkees. It was me, Kenny G, and The Monkees, and it was to tracks, but it was in front of about 70,000 people! It was a really big concert. I was watching the news that night, and the TV commentator said, "The big surprise of the show was Debbie Gibson." That was what it was all about. Here I was, I didn't have a band or anything, and this event really helped launch me in Florida. Obviously, every time I do a promotional event, it isn't in front of 70,000 people, sometimes it is 100 people at a club, or 200 people at a club, but all of that stuff is important.

I'm a performer, and that's what's important. You can talk about being a performer all you want, but until the audience sees you doing it, it doesn't have the same impact. In-store autograph signings in record stores are just as important. I love meeting people, and I love seeing who is buying my records. I want to see who is listening to my music. I can honestly say that "I love my audience." The people who come to my shows, they're there to have fun. They're not "too cool" to dance and scream and have fun, and I love it. They're just into it.

Another thing that I get a big kick out of, is when little kids dress like me. I never intentionally set out to make an image for myself. Just something as simple as the hat and the ripped jeans, it's so flattering to see little kids dressed that way. It's really funny, because my outfits are just something that I throw together from my closet, and now kids are going out wearing it! It's so nice to make somebody happy like that, just by doing what I like to do.

MY VIDEOS

There were five videos that were shot of songs from my first album. It's not unheard of to have five singles off one album, but it is rare that a record company will pay for more than four videos. I don't think that anyone thought that I could talk Atlantic into a fifth video, but I did. I said, "Look, we have a fifth single, I want to have a fifth video." Although we talked them into it, my compilation video had already been released, so it wasn't in-

Debbie Gibson

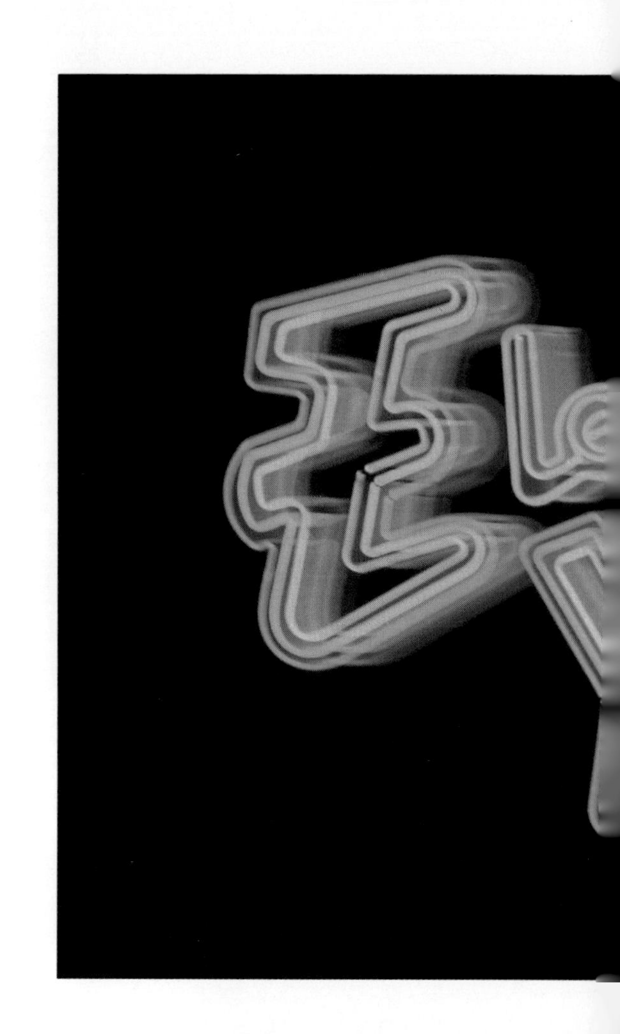

Debbie Gibson

NEW YORK

MG

Music Hall RADIO CITY
DEBBIE GIBSON LIVE IN CONCERT SEPTEMBER 9 - 11 SOLD OUT

cluded. The video was for the song "Staying Together," which is one of my favorite videos. It was shot in concert, filmed in Houston. In a way, people can get the gist of it from watching me do it on my "In Concert" video cassette.

There are some funny shots of me in the "Staying Together" video. One shot has me picking up this spaghetti. It was food that they served at this venue. They can never do spaghetti right. I can't even stand Italian restaurants, forget being able to make a good batch of spaghetti for fifty people! It is like high school cafeteria spaghetti. There's a shot of me with the spaghetti, going: "Mmmmmmm!"

NATURAL WONDER

When I first started releasing records, I swore that I would never do product endorsements. Then Revlon cosmetics approached me to do a series of their "Natural Wonder" make-up ads. I felt I wanted to do it, because the product just goes along with my image, and its like showing kids that I can promote a product that lets me look natural. I don't want to have a bunch of ten-year-old fans dressed up like clowns so they can look like me. I enjoy doing those ads. It is a product that I can genuinely endorse.

I really like the way that they do the ads. They put little quotes by me on them, and the ads are all very "me." It's not like I have to compromise myself in any way. It's just like appearing in a publicity shot in a magazine. Every quote in the ads are things that I've said, and I feel good about the way they're handled. What could be more natural for a teenage girl to promote? Teenage girls and make-up are like a fact of life!

My music is the same way. I like to write about things that everybody can relate to in their everyday lives. I don't sing songs about politics or world issues. I leave that up to the news. That's all too depressing for me. It's not that I don't think about important issues . . . it's just not something I want to sing about. Everyone's meant to make their own kind of music, and I obviously write about everyday lives.

Make-up and music are two things that teenage girls think more about than anything else in the world. I'm glad that there are so many girls who are into my music — and my look!

6

Hitting the Road

After my first album was released, it was time to put together a band, and launch my first concert tour. The "track dates" that I had done were purposeful in establishing an audience for me, but I wanted to go out with a "live" band and really show my audience what I was all about. It was time to hit the road for real!

Choosing the band members was as important as selecting the right dancers for my stage act. I had known Tommy, my lead guitarist, for years. He was the first person that we thought of calling to say, "Do you know some other guys who would be interested in being in my band?" Tommy had been the member of several other bands, so I trusted his opinion.

A lot of people told me that they thought I should get professional touring musicians, but I said, "I don't want to have a band who is identified with other performers." Like, I didn't want to get this one's keyboard player, or that one's guitarist, or something like that. I really wanted my own band. With the band that I have now, I really feel like we're a band, and that we aren't going to go off on our own different directions after "this" tour or "that" event is over. I didn't want a bunch of strangers hired just to play with me for one single tour. I didn't want it to be like that. I wanted young, new faces and fresh musicians, not the same people that everyone's already seen.

After all, I'm a young kid from Long Island. We put together the band basically through the grapevine. Like, Tommy knew Kirk, and Kirk knew Adam, and so on. Well, we put these guys together, and they blew everyone away! They played for the record company, and the executives at Atlantic were just blown away. We put the band together in the fall of 1987.

Our first tour together consisted of college dates. We did about thirty-five college dates, and again I was doing them on the weekends, while I was going to school. These were small concert situations, with audiences of one to three thousand people. The tickets would be available first to college kids, and then to outsiders. It wasn't a highly publicized concert tour, just basically a chance to get out in front of people and to play our music. There was basically no production, just some lights. It was a real good way to get the show together. And it was a great opportunity to let my music just stand up for itself, and not to have the production effects overshadow me. It was up to me to carry the show. I didn't have

anything to fall back on in that situation. There were no lighting effects or anything. We added all that later on. I wanted people to pay attention to the music.

In June 1988, I went out on the road again, and this time around we played thirty-five major dates across America, through July, August, and September. It was the exact same band. But now we had our own stage, lighting, set, and costumes.

For that first tour, Buddy and Keith and I choreographed a couple of the songs, and the rest was totally spontaneous. I had enough theater experience, so I knew how to entertain people, and I just love doing it — and I think that it shows. I'm having fun up there. I think that the second you see someone on-stage who is uncomfortable, you're going to be uncomfortable as well.

But I put 150% of my energy into performing. I remember it was really hot for several of the nights in the summer when I played outdoors. It was ninety degrees and humid in July when I played Houston, Texas. It was so hot that it was crazy, but it was like: "Those kids don't care, they just want to be entertained!" So, I'd go out there in the heat and play for over an hour and a half, and then come off-stage and drink a gallon of water!

Most of the costumes that I wore during that tour were my ideas. For instance, when I sang the 1950's song, "In The Still Of The Night," I wore a sequinned varsity "letter sweater." I went into a store and I saw this sequinned jacket, and I had one with patches on it too. And, I said, "This would look really cool, if it was straight and black, and looked like a letter sweater. Maybe we could put a letter on it." So, I asked the clerk who said, "Oh, I don't know, let me check and see what we can do." So, I said, "Why don't you call and see if it can be done for me. It shouldn't be that big a deal." And, it was done for me. I love everything about the 1950's and that varsity sweater reminds me of that era.

The other thing about me on stage is that I like to have a little pizzaz. I like to look natural and comfortable in what I'm wearing, but I still have to look like I'm a performer. I went with the letter sweater idea, but it was covered with black sequins.

It was perfect for the song "In The Still Of The Night." I'm just in love with '50's music, and that is probably the biggest '50's hit of all times. It was so funny, because I thought of it, and said, "That would be a good thing to do live." And I went into band rehearsal, and I said, "Why don't we try it?" I swear, the first time that we played it, it sounded just like it did in concert. It was really natural, because a lot of the guys in my band had played the song in wedding bands. So they were used to doing it. But we just played it, and I immediately loved it.

We also did "Crocodile Rock" in the show. To me that song just sounds like good old rock and roll music, and again — since that was the first single I ever bought — it was very special to me. Another segment that we added mid-tour in 1988, was a Motown medley. That was my idea as well. I went into one of the hotel offices where I was touring, and I photocopied all these songs that I wanted to do, and then I put them together in a logical order. We were putting that medley together during sound checks. We didn't have it together until the last fifteen dates of the tour, because there just hadn't been enough time to spend on it when we started out. So, we put it together while we were on tour, and did all of the choreography. Keith remembers teaching some of the choreography to the girls by the pool at one of the hotels. That was such a fun segment of the show to put together. While we were working on it, one of the custodians at one of the venues we were at, stopped what he was doing, and hollered to us, "Wow, man, that's happening! I like that!"

To me, all of those classic Motown songs are just fun, upbeat, goodtime songs. I love all of that classic choreography, too. The songs we did were: The Jackson Five's "I Want You Back," "ABC," and "The Love You Save," plus The Supremes' "Stop In The Name Of Love" and "Where Did Our Love Go."

On one of the nights when we played

Radio City Music Hall, I ran all the way up to the balcony! While I was doing the show, I realized there were steps leading from the stage up to the balcony. When I noticed them, my security guards saw me looking at the steps and they were like going, "Don't do it! Don't do it!" Well, I was so hyped up that while the band played, I ran up the side of the Music Hall, and I was able to reach across and shake hands with members of the audience! The kids in the balcony were all leaning over to shake hands with me, and my parents got scared that someone might fall.

The next night I did it again, and when I got to the top, I discovered that a security guard had been stationed there, and he almost got knocked over by the kids. The kids started pushing him down, and he was hanging over the rail! But, I had to do it. It was such a great feeling. Who expects to sit in the balcony and have an artist come up and shake your hand? The spotlight followed me and I loved being in the audience like that. I felt like I was part of the audience! Everyone was looking around and going, "Where is Debbie? Where is Debbie? Oh, there she is!" It was a riot.

I always get mad when they put barriers up in front of the stage. I love being right there, and having the kids right there with me.

During this particular concert tour, I pulled a lot of people up on stage with me when I sang "We Could Be Together." What was really fun, was when we filmed the concert "live," for the video cassette that we released. We filmed it in Pittsburgh, and it was really a weird show, because to film it, all of the house lights had to be turned on. It ended up looking dark on tape, but all the house lights were on. I said to the audience, "I feel like I'm doing this show in my living room." I could see everybody's faces throughout the whole show. It was fun, though, and really different.

The last show of the tour was the funniest. It was at R.P.I. Field House in Rochester, New York. Since it was the final show, everyone in the band and crew was playing jokes on everyone else. When the opening band was playing, I snuck out through security to the monitor board, and started singing a harmony vocal with the band. They were all looking around, trying to figure out where this extra voice was coming from.

Then, the guys from my band started taking their gear and their instruments off-stage while they were playing. It was so funny. Throughout the whole tour, we had this joke about "heavy salad." When something was intense, instead of saying, "Oh, that's really heavy stuff," we would say, "That's heavy salad." I said to some of the crew members, you should come out on stage with a huge salad, give it to me, and I'll dump it on someone's head. So, they took the idea, but they dumped the salad on my head! They chased me all over the stage with this big bowl of salad from the caterer. It was huge!

Then, during the song "Shake Your Love," there was what we call the " 'Shake' break," where I go off stage and change my outfit. Then, one of the background singers, Chris, walks back on stage, and that's the sign that I'm dressed and finished with my costume change. So, we dressed my sister Michele up in a wig and a black dress, and she came walking on stage instead of Chris, and no one knew who she was! The band was going, "Who is she?" And, to top it off, I left the band up there on stage during the " 'Shake' break" for ten minutes. Usually I'm changed in two or three minutes; instead, I left then up there to fend for themselves! I wanted to see how long Keith could work that audience. For ten minutes he was dancing and the drummer was nearly getting blisters on his fingers from playing so long! It was a really funny show!

We did all kinds of things like that. When we came out for the encore, I played the drums. I can play the drums just a little bit for fun, by ear. I'm terrible, but I love it. It's fun to bang on the drums, and that's something that eventually I'd like to learn how to do. I forgot what song to play, and all of a sudden, I'm playing a beat, and I yelled to the band and asked what song to play. It was such a funny show!

Another time when I was at Radio City Music Hall, it was to tape the game show "Hollywood Squares." That was such a fun event. I got twenty tickets for my friends to sit in the audience, and they all came. The funniest thing was the fact that I was so nervous. I don't get nervous on stage when I perform, but as soon as you take me out of my context, I'm uncomfortable. It's hard to be on a game show. You have to think on your feet, and come up with funny things, and it was really difficult! I was thinking, "I can't believe that I was so nervous on this game show." It was such a really weird experience, because I hadn't ever done anything like that. But I ended up having a blast.

I also did the show again, and I taped an entire week of shows. A lot of people said to me, "Oh, I don't know if it's such a good idea to do a game show." I said, "Hey, I know I'm a singer and writer, but I also like to have some other kinds of fun." I think that people enjoy watching you make a fool out of yourself sometimes on television. It was funny. I also sang on the show the week that I was on it. I think that there is a whole audience out there who watch game shows at dinner time, and for me it was an opportunity to reach a whole different audience, which was kind of a cool thing to do. I had a lot of fun during the taping sessions of "Hollywood Squares," both in New York City, and in California.

Two years before I appeared on the show as a guest, I stumbled onto the set of the "Hollywood Squares." The show was being taped on the beach in Hollywood, Florida, when I was there promoting my twelve-inch single, "Only In My Dreams." I couldn't get tickets to "Hollywood Squares," so I crashed the set, and Olympic gymnast Mitch Gaylord was on the show. He was my big heartthrob at the time, and I just had to meet him! I was always gutsy like that: I hid behind a rock behind the set, and I waited for the right moment, and when they took a commercial break, I hopped over a barrier and, in front of the whole audience, I ran up to Mitch and said, "Can I take a picture of you?" It was really funny. When I took my picture, I handed him a copy of my twelve-inch single, and I said, "Oh, by the way — I just did this record. Here's a copy."

When I was little, I always liked to watch game shows on television, and I always wanted to be on "The Joker's Wild." I used to love that show! I used to watch "Bowling For Dollars," and "The Price Is Right," too. Those were my other two favorites.

One of the most thrilling things that I have ever done was to appear as part of the Atlantic Records 40th Anniversary show at Madison Square Garden. The "Atlantic Records 40th Anniversary" TV special starred all of the label's biggest acts from the beginning of the company, to the 1980's. It included a lot of their great R&B artists: Roberta Flack, Ben E. King, and Ruth Brown. Keith Stewart said, "I knew that I had landed in the land of the stars when I saw Miss Roberta Flack sitting at the piano singing "Killing Me Softly." She was just incredible. I just love that song, "Killing Me Softly."

The show also included several great rock bands, like Yes and Foreigner. Led Zeppelin was the big climax, and they performed last on the bill as the grand finale. It was really difficult to get up in front of that crowd, because they were all there to see Led Zeppelin. The concert went on all day long, and some of the acts got "booed" off the stage. Some members of the audience just wanted to see Led Zeppelin, so it took a lot of nerve to get up on stage.

I looked at the event as a real challenge. I said, "Let's see if I can really turn this audience around." And when I came out on stage, I didn't get booed. There was applause, but it wasn't enthusiastic like it was my audience. It was evening, and the event was being televised "live" via satellite at this point. I received what I would call "polite applause." By the end of my set, it was like a standing ovation! I was really thrilled that I had pulled that off. It was especially a challenge, because I

Meeting Phil Collins at Atlantic Records' 40th Anniversary concert at Madison Square Garden, 1988.

With director Jim Yukich and Mike Rutherford of Genesis, at Atlantic's 40th.

With Billy Joel, backstage at Madison Square Garden, at the Elton John concert, 1988.

On-stage at Madison Square Garden: my hands on the same keyboard as Elton John's!

followed the group Yes. The funniest thing was that it was an emotionally exhausting thing, because it was "live," and it was telecast to millions of people all over the world. I knew that my friends were at home having parties, and watching it. As soon as I hit the stage, I don't have a nervous bone in my body, but the waiting around was nerve-wracking. I was emotionally exhausted by the time I got up on stage, and then I put every ounce of energy that I had into my performance. Afterwards, I was absolutely ready to go home. I'm not one to hang around and chit-chat. I arrived at Madison Square Garden about a half an hour before I went on stage, and I left about a half hour after I was finished. I talked to the press, and I posed for some photos with some people, and was out of there.

Someone came up to me when I was ready to leave and said, "Could you come over her please, I have a photo set up with you and Robert Plant." And I said, "I'm sorry, but I just can't, I've got to get out of here, I'm exhausted!"

I performed three songs that night. I did "Staying Together," "Foolish Beat," and a medley of "Out Of The Blue," "Shake Your Love," and "Only In My Dreams."

Another time that I performed in Madison Square Garden, came in October 1988. I went to see Elton John's concert, and I ended up on stage, performing with Elton, and with Billy Joel!

Before Elton's show, I had arranged to go backstage and meet him. When I met him, he said to me, "Would you like to come up and do a song with me and Billy?" — meaning

Billy Joel!!! And I said, "Are you kidding me?! Of course!!!" Thank goodness I dressed decently, and wasn't in jeans and a T-shirt.

I was with my family and friends, and a couple of songs before the last song, right at the encores — I went backstage. Elton gave me a great introduction. He is one of the nicest performers I have ever met — he is just so nice! He was really gracious and he was much nicer than he had to be, which was really incredible. There were so many people backstage, and he had a show to think about, and yet he was really nice. The song that we performed — Elton and Billy and I — was "Lucy In The Sky With Diamonds." Billy Joel had his own keyboard set up on stage, because that had already been arranged. So Elton said, "Well, sit at my keyboard with me." I sat at his keyboard and just kept looking down at my hands on the keyboard next to his. I remember thinking to myself, "Our hands are on the same keyboard together — I don't believe it!' Elton is one of the greats! It was an amazing experience. I just had so much fun. Again, I didn't have a nervous bone in my body — it was just so much fun! I loved it.

That night, I forgot to tell Elton that the first single that I ever bought was "Crocodile Rock." And I was going to bring it, and have him autograph it, but I couldn't find it in my room! What an incredible evening that was — performing with my two idols — Elton John *AND* Billy Joel!

Taking a bow with two of my idols: Billy Joel and Elton John.

CALHOUN

7

High School Chronicles

While all of this was going on in my career, I was finishing my senior year in high school. It got really crazy, to say the least. Right when I returned to school in the fall of 1987, at the beginning of twelfth grade, is when it really was hectic.

It was a little crazy in two respects. First of all because, I would go into school and everyone would ask me to sign autographs for their cousins and sisters and brothers. At the same time, there was a group who would remark sarcastically, "Oh, there she is — the famous singer." A lot of the kids I went to school with seemed to resent my success.

There were three groups of people in my school: (1) those who were resentful, (2) those who were star struck, and (3) my friends. The only people that I paid attention to were my friends. That worked out well. My friends were always my friends, because they could appreciate how much work I was putting into my singing career.

Obviously, there were teachers who were also resentful. They had the attitude: "Oh who does this kid think she is, making records, and thinking she can come to school whenever she wants." I don't know what they thought when they heard I was traveling. Did they think that I was away — floating on a raft with a pina colada in my hand or something?

I was working! They didn't realize that it was work. They didn't realize it until they saw it with their own eyes. Even when we got tickets for some of the teachers to attend one of my concerts they were still skeptical. After they saw me in concert, they finally really realized, and admitted, "Now we see just how hard she works on stage."

I couldn't even get credit for gym class, even though I was dancing five hours a day! So it wasn't like I got away with anything. If anything, I did more work than I would have had to do. For instance, I had four health textbooks, instead of one — to make sure that I didn't miss anything while I was in class. I still had to take the same tests, I still had to take the same finals, the same Regents tests. Nobody could justify saying that I didn't work hard, but there were still a couple of comments made to me with regard to having received "star treatment."

But I had it in my mind to stay in a normal public high school. I didn't want to get tutors, I wanted to stay with my friends. Everyone has to go to school and experience things like rivalries, and jealousies. Cheerleaders experience it all of the time, just because they're pretty and they're popular — they take abuse for it. I think that everyone has to go through something like that. Everyone has to go through dealing with difficulties, especially during their teenage years. So, I just kind of joked about it, and I kept my concentration focused on what it was that I wanted to accomplish.

As far as my work went, I just kept up with it, and I went through the normal graduation ceremony with everyone else. But even that was a little weird, because I had to have security guards with me. The members of the press wanted to come, but we hired one photographer, and had someone videotape it. We told the press that we would take care of photographing the ceremony, and supply them

Girls just want to have fun! That's my favorite toy that we're dancing with — my '57 Ford!

with videotape or still photographs. I insisted that it not turn into a big publicity event, or a three-ring circus. I just wanted to have my graduation day, just like any other normal high school senior. We did it that way, and it worked out really well.

Afterward, we had a big graduation party for me and my friends. It was held at my Aunt Linda's house. We couldn't have it at our house, because we lived only one block from the school, and everyone would have seen where we lived. Right after the graduation ceremony, we took off for my aunt's house. It was just my friends and my family who were there.

When the question of college came up, I decided not to continue school. By this point, I knew that I was doing exactly what I wanted to do career-wise, and that my work experiences were far more valuable to me. There are colleges for music, but you can't touch the instruments or recording equipment until the second semester. I'll say this to anyone: "The only way you're going to learn about music — whether it's engineering, producing, or singing — is to do it." It's not something that I think you can learn in school. You can learn what "hertz" means or what "DB's" are, but you can't learn the kind of natural instincts that creative people have out of a book. I learned by experimenting.

Whenever I bought a new piece of recording equipment, I hid the manuals and instruction booklets from myself. I refused to read the manuals in the beginning, I wanted to learn for myself what every control did. And that's basically what I did.

A lot of people go to college to figure out what it is that they want to do with their lives, and for the social aspects. Well, I've met more people in the last year than I can ever keep track of, and I'm surrounded by people that I love. And, most important of all — I'm doing exactly what it is that I want to do with my life. It's not like I have to go to college to learn what I want to do with my life — I'm already doing it!

You learn how to do something by doing it. I did take some acting classes, but I learned more about acting by just getting up on stage. College is good for finding yourself, and for people who need to have some time away from home, but it's not right for me. Even if I had gone to college, I don't think that I would have moved away from home. Like I mentioned before, the young side of me is still very young. I'm very independent in some ways, and very dependent in others. I have strong opinions and ideas, but at the same

Having my favorite junk food at The Hard Rock Cafe in New York City — a burger and a shake!

time, I still can't cook more than a bowl of spaghetti by myself!

I'm just not ready to move out of the house, and be on my own. I'm around strangers so much that I still love the comfort of coming home to my parents and sisters. Moving away from home is just not what I want to do at the moment.

Although I'm not interested in attending college, there are several classes that I would like to take. I would like to study more about foreign languages, and about film production. Film production is something that I've learned a lot about just by being on the set of my videos, and I find it fascinating. For the time being, I've purchased some foreign language tapes, and I sit and listen to them. That's one way of learning. There are ways of learning on your own as well. It's not for the piece of paper at the end of the class, I want to learn, because I *want* to learn.

One of the highlights of my life was getting my drivers license, and my car! It took me so long to get my drivers license, because I just never had time. I would learn to drive, and then I would go away for three months. Then I'd come back, and I'd not be comfortable with it. I didn't find that it was "just like riding a bicycle." You still have to get reacquainted with the car when you're a beginner driver.

My sisters were teasing me, and going: "What's wrong with you? We were camping out in front of the Department of Motor Vehicles on the eve of our sixteenth birthdays to get our permits — and the night before our seventeenth birthdays to get our licenses!" Meanwhile, I didn't get my driver's license until I was over eighteen!

Getting the license was so funny. I passed the road test on the first time out. I had to take it in the rain, and that was the first time I had driven in the rain. But I passed it, and I bought a 1957 Ford Fairlane, which I love to death! I love everything about the '50's, and to me, there's nothing like an old car. Old cars are so much fun, and I just love it — it's the ultimate cruising machine!

In Central Park — reading between the lines!

EL

8

Electric Youth

The title song of the "Electric Youth" album is very meaningful to me. It is about taking young people seriously. I guess for a long time people didn't take me very seriously. Even now, there are some people who don't take me seriously. Really the song is just about people treating young people like people, as opposed to saying, "Oh, he's just a kid."

I've met some brilliant young people. Just look at the Olympic games. There are Olympic gymnasts who are only fifteen and sixteen, and who are on top of the world — the best in the world! There really is no such thing as: "the older you are the better you are," or "you're too young to do this." There is no such thing as that, and this is what my song's about.

The video that I made for that song was very special for me as well, because I co-directed it with Jim Yukich. I basically wanted to do something really phenomenal. I wanted to show people that I could dance — or to try to dance at least! I've taken dancing lessons, and I knew I could move, but it was a matter of working real hard at it to get really sharp and everything.

For some reason, I had always envisioned the video taking place in a castle. Because, in the beginning of the song, there is a trumpet fanfare. Obviously, the dancing had to take place somewhere. I figured that I'd go on that theme, and have a dungeon and the whole bit. That was my concept. I'm really proud of that video, and it's my favorite. Barry Lather choreographed it. He's worked with Janet Jackson, and Sting, and he's also really young. I didn't have any idea of how young he was when we called him. I didn't know if he was black or white, or young or old. I just knew of him from the work that he had done. And, come to find out, he's twenty-two years old!

When I found that out, I said, "Great! We're doing 'Electric Youth,' choreographed by someone who's twenty-two years old, and my concept — an eighteen-year-old! I worked on the choreography with Barry for a week, and really worked hard. I felt good about it.

My second album, "Electric Youth" was recorded in May, June, October, November, and December of 1988. Fred Zarr produced four of the songs, he and I co-produced one of the songs, and the other six cuts on the album I produced by myself. Here is a cut-by-cut explanation of each of the cuts:

"WHO LOVES YA BABY?"

I would not have even come up with that kind of an idea for a song if I hadn't heard that Olivia Newton-John was looking for songs for her new album. When I heard that, for some reason, I decided to write something for her. I was thinking, and I just started singing this song. As it turned out, she decided to pass on the song. This happens with my songs all the time.

I originally heard about Olivia needing songs through my sister Karen. But Olivia said that it just wasn't right for that particular album. I could understand that. I was just listening to the album the other night, and my song really didn't fit in with what was going on in that album.

When I was submitting it, I was told, "You're crazy, you ought to keep that song for yourself." But I really thought it would be good for her. I could just hear her singing it. I was always a big Olivia Newton John fan. But I ended up doing it, and it ended up being one of my favorite things from the album. It was a song that I could really get "vocal" with, and really sing on it.

"LOST IN YOUR EYES"

"Lost In Your Eyes" I wrote on a little pad of assignment paper. I wrote that one day after school. I remember sitting down and writing it.

I performed this song on my summer 1988 concert tour, even before it was released. It got a good reaction then, and it was a good guide to see how people were going to respond to it.

When I first wrote it, I was certain that I wanted this to be the first single off the album. It ended up becoming a huge Number One pop hit, and stayed at the top of the charts for three weeks. I was thrilled!

What was also really exciting on that song, was that, this was the first time I had ever played "live" piano on a record. After all those years of piano lessons, I was really excited to hear myself on the radio, playing the piano.

I remember that several of the radio stations ended up getting copies of "Lost In Your Eyes" before it was officially released. I was so excited that there was this big hype over my new album and my new single! I knew that there would be a certain amount of acceptance, but I didn't realize that people were going to get that hyped. I was really excited about that, because every radio station wanted to be the first station in their area to have a copy of it. It immediately became the Number One most-requested new song on the charts. I couldn't have been happier!

Although I had started my recording career with a dance hit, I didn't have any apprehension about releasing a ballad as the first single off my album. I think that ballads really show what an artist can do — more than anything, vocally. Ballads are more long-lasting hits than dance music. People just seem to remember them forever. I always listen to the radio when they have the "Dedication Hour," and I constantly hear people requesting "Lost In Your Eyes." It feels great when I hear that song dedicated to people. I love that! I'll be in a bad mood, and I'll be listening to the radio, and I'll hear, "This one's going out from Joe to Sue, and from Linda to Carl . . ." and then my song is played. That makes me feel great to hear that happen. Isn't that what it's all about?

"LOVE IN DISGUISE"

"Love In Disguise" is another song that I performed in concert before the album was out. Sometimes two people break up because they think it's time for a change. Then, both people walk around pretending that everything's fine when, in fact, they want to get back together. That's what this song's all about.

I had the chorus/hook to this song for months, because I lost the verses. Anyway, I wrote new verses, found the old ones, and I decided that I liked the new ones much better anyway. So, everything worked out for the best!

"HELPLESSLY IN LOVE"

"Helplessly In Love" reminds me of the '60's. I wrote this song about the same time that I wrote "Lost In Your Eyes." Again, this is a self-explanatory love song about someone who is — you guessed it — helplessly in love. I would like to explain one line: "I can't see clearly even though the sun's been lifted from your eyes . . ." I guess what I'm trying to say is that love blinds you when it's around,

With Mom in Stockholm, April 1989. I love Europe!

but still leaves you blinded and confused when it's gone.

"SILENCE SPEAKS A THOUSAND WORDS"

This song begins with a sort of classical or madrigal feeling. I think that my classical training is coming through, subconsciously, in that arrangement. When I hear this song, I think of a quiet, peaceful beach. I learned how to play that flute solo, and I performed that part in concert a few times.

This song has one of my favorite arrangements. It is very musical to me. I think that this is my favorite arrangement.

"SHOULD'VE BEEN THE ONE"

"Should've Been The One" is a song that I was thinking about recording for my first album. I wrote the song when I was fourteen, but it just didn't fit on the first album. It would have been one of those "Which one doesn't belong here?" situations. It didn't go along with the whole dance/pop format of my "Out Of The Blue" album.

This is real rock and roll song. When we were remixing it, the engineer I was working with, Bob Rosa, said, "This sounds like 'Debbie Gibson Meets the "E" Street Band!' " That's what it sounds like to me, too. It's very rock and roll, and I love rock and roll. But, I love all kinds of music, but there's nothing like a good rock and roll song!

"Should've Been The One" gets a great response in concert. The song itself is about that one person you always had your heart set on, but was unobtainable.

"ELECTRIC YOUTH"

I explained the meaning of this song at the beginning of this chapter. I owe a lot to my family and teachers for helping to develop my creative side and for teaching me and many other kids how to channel their energy into worthwhile and creative projects.

"NO MORE RHYME"

This song marks the first time that Fred Zarr produced a song for me, without my having done a demo first. I was a little nervous about it at first, because I thought, "Oh-oh, is he going to hear what I'm hearing in my mind?" It ended up that I loved what he did! It's perfect — right on the nose . . . exactly.

Again, this is a very vocal song, and it really gives me a chance to sing. This is a song about how the consistency or the "rhythm" of a relationship will keep it going, even though the substance, or the "rhyme" is gone. The line, "waiting for the other shoe to drop" is like waiting for the last note of a scale to be played, or waiting for something to go wrong in a relationship, because everything is going too smoothly.

"OVER THE WALL"

"Over The Wall" I produced and arranged myself. When I was mixing the music for my "In Concert" video, I decided that I wanted to record a new demo. I hadn't demoed a new song for a while, and I had written this song when I was on tour, and I really wanted to make a demo tape of it.

I demoed it, and then ended up using some of those basic tracks on the finished recording to the song. I did go back and rerecord some of the parts on it, but some of the original tracks are on it as well. I really like the string arrangement on it.

This is another of my songs that I wrote with someone else in mind. I submitted it to Madonna, and she turned it down! I thought that it sounded very Madonna-like. But, it was actually more like the old Madonna, than the new Madonna sound. Madonna definitely has changed. Again, her response was that this song didn't quite fit with the project she was doing. And, again this is true. Her "Like A Prayer" album is very different sounding. But still that song really does have an old Madonna feeling to it. That was the first time that I could hear Madonna's influence in my music.

I love the music that Madonna did on her first album. I love "Borderline" and "Holiday" and songs like that. It's fun music. It's pure pop music. No one got overanalytical doing it. It sounded very spontaneous.

"WE COULD BE TOGETHER"

"We Could Be Together" is my favorite song, out of all of the songs I have ever written. Again, just like Motown songs — this song is fun, just a feel-good song. I like the lyrics to it. It has a good message. It is about not stereotyping people.

This is another song that I performed on my 1988 summer tour. I did an eight minute version of this song in concert, and I had the audience on their feet singing the song with me, "We could be together, for a while." To me, it's like a singalong. This is the song that I was performing when I ran up the steps at Radio City Music Hall to shake hands with the audience in the balcony.

The song tells a story. You know, when people look down on you because of who you go out with, because of the clique they're in, or because of some stereotype? You should do what you want to to be happy in the end. Don't listen to other people when it comes to your happiness.

"SHADES OF THE PAST"

This is another one of the songs that Fred Zarr produced. Again, I just gave him a piano and vocal tape, because I didn't have time to do the demo. I originally heard it as more a rock ballad, with live drums and everything, and he came up with this really jazzy arrangement. The first time I heard it was over the phone, and I was going, "I hate it! I hate it! What am I going to do?" So, I told him that wasn't quite what I had in mind. But, I said that I would give it a chance, and I would try to maintain an open mind. He played the track that he came up with, and I sang to it — and it felt great! It was something totally different for me. That's why I like working with other people, because they can show you different ways to things. I ended up loving the way this song sounds. It felt really jazzy, and I had never done anything like that.

My "Electric Youth" album was released in January 1989, and it only took five weeks to climb to Number One! Again, my first album never went to Number One. I think the highest it got was to Number Six or Seven. Even

With Maria Shriver and cast of the TV show "Main Street."

though it sold three million copies, it lingered on the chart.

It was outrageous to think that my album was the best selling album of the week! I was thrilled. I mean, it's not the be-all and end-all of life, but it sure felt great! But, I don't just want to have the hottest album of the week, I want to have a career that has longevity and growth. It was even more incredible to have the Number One single and the Number One album on the charts for the same weeks! How could that not feel incredible!?!

I've done a couple more videos from the "Electric Youth" album as well. My "No More Rhyme" video was very different for me. First of all, the main focus was me, which is new for my videos. I don't like to do that. If you watch all my videos, I always have a lot of people in them, and a lot of close-ups of other people, and I'm kind of singing throughout the other action on camera. But, it was my concept that "No More Rhyme" would be more effective being just me, with a lot of close-ups, to really drive home the point of the song. I wanted the song to be the main focus of this video. If you see me, I definitely look older in it. I didn't do it intentionally, but if you're singing a mature ballad, you're going to look a little more mature. Some people look at it and say, "Oh, my God! You look almost 25!"

It's funny, because I'm not really doing anything different in the video, it's just that I'm not bopping around, and I would look much younger doing that. I think the final outcome is a very effective video to illustrate this song.

A lot of people compare Tiffany and me. I remember the first time I met her. We were both on the set of the television show "Top Of The Pops" in Hollywood. At the time I was doing "Shake Your Love," and she was doing "I Think We're Alone Now." I thought that immediately people were going to start rumors about us having this kind of rivalry. Well, I didn't want her to think that there was any kind of a rivalry, either. So what I did was, I got her a card, and said to her, "It's nice to see another teen on the charts." And, it's true, because, like I said, I'm such a believer in "youth" that it was great. Tiffany and I don't have a rivalry, we have more of a camaraderie. I am really happy about her success. Our music is really different, so there never was any competition.

I wrote Tiffany a letter, and we exchanged phone numbers, but we haven't had the opportunity to really talk at length yet. It's just because we're both so busy. We do run into each other now and then, and she's really nice.

Tiffany and I have a lot in common. That goes without saying. We have so much in common to talk about — school, and juggling our careers as teenagers.

I love the fact that I get to travel around and meet people in other countries. Two of my favorite places are England and Japan. I remember my first impression of London, and that it seemed like everyone dressed in black! Everyone over there wants to look very sophisticated. I remember watching a TV show where they were making fun at the idea of women putting on sneakers in New York City, to wear to get to the train station, and then changing into high heels at the office. You don't have to be fashionable every second. Comfort is number one here! Those were my first impressions of London.

When I met everyone over there, I found them all to be very nice. They really do have a dry sense of humor in England. It's funny. What I like is the fact that some of the television shows are really funny, and they're really into that silly sense of humor. It's so cool over there.

There is also great shopping over there. I bought my prom dress in London. I only had like a half hour between interviews, and I ran into Hyper Hyper, which I love. It's all different shops — like a big flea market. I also bought a great brown leather jacket over there.

While I was in London, I went to the theater to see the musicals *Phantom Of The Opera* and *Chess.* They were both great pro-

With my grandfather and his brothers, in my "Electric Youth" video.

I believe that my family is the most important thing to me.

ductions. The first concert that I did in London was at a 3,000 seat theater, and the audience was great. I enjoyed doing that show a lot. The fans over there get really into singers and performers they like. It's cool how the records there often have free posters with them. My British fans are really dedicated, which is really nice.

Once I got into a crowd of overly enthusiastic fans in London, and I didn't think that I was going to escape! Someone was pulling at my scarf, someone else was pulling at my hat. I was with my mom and David Salidor, my publicist, and they suddenly realized that they had to act as my security guards. It got crazy, but it was fun!

I also performed at The Prince's Trust Gala concert. And I got to meet Princess Diana and Prince Charles. That was really exciting. It was exciting in the sense that they're royalty and everything, but at the same time, I reacted like myself meeting normal people. I never really got into the concept of royalty, or of celebrities, or what makes someone better than someone else. It doesn't make them better than someone else, but it's kind of weird. I'll tell you what was really going on in my mind, was what they have to deal with in their everyday lives. It kind of freaked me out. It was like, "If I think that Madonna or Bruce Springsteen have problems with their celebrity status, think of what Princess Diana and Prince Charles have to deal with!" Waiting for them to arrive that evening, we kept getting updates on their progress: "They're ten minutes away," "They're five minutes away," "They're two minutes away," They're getting out of the car," and so on. The security was really intense. I felt bad in a sense, because it's not like they even chose that kind of lifestyle, they were born into it. It must be really difficult.

They were both very nice. Prince Charles was kind of funny and witty. What was really funny was, that I was the first one to perform, so I was in my performance outfit, which was the cut off jeans and black vest that I wear when I do "Electric Youth." They told me to just wear that because I didn't have time to change. Here we are, and there are all of these people in gowns, and I'm in my shorts. Princess Diana said to me, "Oh, you must be more comfortable than the rest of us!" I thought that was really funny and cute!

There were several other people on the show: Roseanna Arquette, Paula Abdul, The Pasadenas, Mica Paris — who is great — and Sean Connery. In fact, Sean Connery was part of the receiving line. He came right after Charles and Diana. He was definitely treated like royalty.

Steve Wright was there, and he had us all cracking up while we were waiting to meet Prince Charles and Princess Diana. It was a different kind of line-up. It was like the "New Generation Show," it wasn't a rock show. It was more like a pop show. It was an incredible experience for me. I did "Lost In Your Eyes" at a grand piano with a full orchestra. That was just incredible. "Electric Youth" I danced to, so I had to lip sync. I know that a lot of people lip sync on television, but I hate it. I hate it more than anything, because the audience knows when you're lip syncing. When I sat down at the piano, I thought to myself, "I'm doing something real." Singing "live" at the piano made up for having to lip sync through the choreography of "Electric Youth."

Sitting there at the piano, while the orchestra played, reminded me of being at the Metropolitan Opera House in Lincoln Center.

Addressing the kids in the WINGS program at my old elementary school, spring 1989.

On the set of my "Electric Youth" video.

It was just like I was back at the Met!

For the "Electric Youth" number, we had fifteen dancers from England, and Buddy and Keith worked with them on the choreography. The reason that I had to lip sync was because there was too much movement in the choreography to mike the number properly. The concert was held to raise money for youth causes, so the idea of using "Electric Youth" to open the show was excellent.

My last European trip, which included visits to Germany, Italy, and France, was also fun. I documented the whole thing on videotape. Unfortunately, my last trip to Europe had to be cut short by three days, because my wisdom teeth were bothering me. We tried to avoid going to a foreign dentist, but we finally gave in in Rome.

My mom and I decided that I had better see a dentist, because the tooth had me in pain, it was giving me a headache, it was putting pressure on my eye, and my eye was blurry. It was ridiculous. We walked into the dentist's office, and right there was a liquor cabinet next to the dentist chair! My mom was just on the floor she was laughing so hard. I kept saying, "Mom, don't lose it on me! Please, I'm in pain. Don't do this to me!" She was just hysterical about the liquor cabinet. Finally, she said, "Excuse me, what's the whiskey for?" And the dentist says, "In case anybody gets nervous!" After that I decided to get home to my regular dentist, as soon as possible.

The dentist in Rome didn't end up doing anything, except to prescribe antibiotics for me. I was having trouble explaining to him what I was allergic to, and he thought I was trying to tell him that I couldn't have any antibiotics. Then we tried to explain it to him again, and this time around he thought that all I could have was antibiotics. It was a real comedy of errors. It was pretty funny.

Of all of the places that I have traveled to outside of America, I really loved Japan. I especially love the people over there. They are just so polite. They bow to you when they meet you, and they really respect music and musicians. When my "Electric Youth" album came out in Japan, it immediately sold more that "Out Of The Blue" ever sold.

I was also impressed by Japanese television shows. I did a "live" TV show, and they had a different set for every act, and there were like fifteen different acts! During the commercial break, there would be about fifty technicians running around moving bushes and furniture.

I was so impressed by Japan that I went out and bought a Japanese language tape. I would love to be able to have in-depth conversations with some of the people in Japan that I met, because they're so nice. Everyone over there is so meticulous and really organized. It is really an incredible country. It's no wonder that they invent all of these wonderful electronic things!

In January 1989, I was one of the cohosts of "The American Music Awards," along with Anita Baker, Kenny Rogers, and Rod Stewart. That was a really exciting evening for me. I like to be able to appear on a program like that, and show people that I'm not just a singer, that I can get up in front of an audience and speak confidently and naturally. Because, people sometimes assume: "Oh, she's just a stupid blonde pop singer." I like to be able to show people different sides of me, and this particular television special gave me an opportunity to show off another side of my performing persona. I had so much fun doing that show, especially since I can distinctly remember driving my family crazy whenever that show was telecast when I was growing up. I would announce to my family, " 'The American Music Awards' are on TV tonight, nobody can go anywhere or do anything tonight, because we've all got to watch this show!" For as long as I can remember, I always sat in front of the television and watched all three hours of that show, every year. I was just always so into watching that show, to see my favorite pop singers and rock stars compete for the top honors.

Now I realize that it is a difficult job choosing a "winner" on a show like that. It's like comparing apples and oranges. You shouldn't really have to choose between Whitney Houston and Belinda Carlysle. The great thing about music is that you can own both their albums, and enjoy them both equally. Whitney and Belinda are totally different, yet those were the two girls I was up against in the category I was nominated in. All three of us are different. I didn't really care if I won or not. All of my concentration was focused on doing a good job as co-host, and as a performer. Again, a lot of people that night sang to tracks or did lip syncing, but my band and I performed "live." I think that my performance on the show that night did a lot to promote my album and my "Lost In Your Eyes" single, because they had just been released at that time. After that, people seemed to have a new respect for me and my music.

That was an exciting evening, and it was such fun to be part of that. It was really something, being on stage, and looking out to the front row, and seeing George Michael, Whitney Houston, Hall and Oates, and all of these other stars sitting there. I mean, these are people whom I admire, and I loved being up there in front of them!

I wasn't at all nervous that evening, especially during the performing segments. When it comes to performing my songs, I can't wait to get out there and start singing. But the first time that I came out on stage to introduce something, I was a little bit nervous.

That day we hired a make-up artist, and at the last minute he couldn't get into the auditorium because of the heavy security. About an hour before the show I realized that I had to do my own make-up. Professional make-up people were provided backstage for anyone who wanted their services, but it was so crowded that I decided to do my own make-up for the show. Here I was in this little trailer, with a little pocket mirror, doing my make-up. I was thinking to myself, "This is the last thing I needed to happen to me a half hour before the show!' But, it ended up turning out O.K. I

With Olivia Newton John at The American Music Awards, January 1989. I originally wrote the song "Who Loves Ya?" with Olivia in mind.

still didn't like the way that I did my make-up that night. It was almost right, but not quite. That's why I'm not a professional make-up artist.

The security was really intense that night. We all had little laminated passes to get in and out of the auditorium. When I went out to the trailer at one point, I left my pass behind. When it came time to go back into the auditorium, the security guards wouldn't let me back in without my pass. So I said, "But you don't understand, I'm one of the hosts of the show!" They still made me go and get a laminated pass before I could get in.

I was recently awarded a plaque by ASCAP. I tied with Bruce Springsteen as "Songwriter Of The Year!" That was one of the most exciting evenings in my entire career. I was thrilled to be recognized as a songwriter. Again, here I was sitting among songwriters whom I admire. People who won awards that night included George Michael, Richard Marx, Diane Warren, and some really great songwriters. I was really choked up during the presentation.

One situation where I really get nervous is at those awards presentations. I get nervous about what I'm going to say when I get to the podium. I got up there, and I got really choked up. I really don't usually have to get up on stage and make a speech. Sometimes even the most heartfelt sentences of appreciation can sound corny. Even though you are sincere about what you are saying, it can come out like a stiff and insincere cliché. Somehow that evening I lost track of what I thought I was going to say, and I ended up adlibing. I even dragged my mom and dad up there with me to receive the award, because I felt that they were so much a part of everything. They were going, "No, no, no!" and I said, "Come on, you're going up there with me!"

The fact that that particular awards show isn't televised, and that it doesn't have any media hype, made it much more meaningful to me. It made it into a really nice event. The whole point of it was to honor the songwriters, among other songwriters. It was a really memorable evening.

When I was on tour in 1988, I got to meet George Michael and attend one of his concerts. Fortunately, our tours coincided in such a way that I had a few days off, when he was performing. We just did a little re-routing in my itinerary, and I hopped over to Detroit to catch his show. I had to see him "live." When I was in the ninth grade, I won tickets to see him as part of the group Wham!, on a radio station contest. I remember, when I first heard Wham!, I came home from being out with my friends, and I turned on MTV, and I saw Wham! doing "Wake Me Up Before You Go Go." When I saw that their name was Wham!, I thought, "What an odd name for a rock group!" I said, "Mom, you have to see this new group called Wham! They're really young and fun, and their song is so catchy." I still love the song "Wake Me Up Before You Go Go," it's such a fun song. It's almost like an old Motown song. We had originally put it in our Motown medley, but took it out because it really wasn't a Motown song, so it didn't quite fit.

George Michael is just a great artist, and his "live" show is one of the best that I've ever seen. I got to go backstage and meet him! He is really nice. He's very humble and friendly. Those are the kind of people who last in this business, and not the people who get all full of themselves in a week. George was so nice and normal to talk to. I was really excited to meet him!

As a host of The American Music Awards. My co-hosts were Anita Baker, Kenny Rogers, and Rod Stewart. Backstage with Michael Jackson (right).

With Dick Clark on the set of "American Bandstand."

9

Reading Between the Lines

Although I love having the opportunity to travel all over the world, I'm pretty much a "home" oriented kind of person. I love to travel, because I love to perform for people everywhere. But, other than that, traveling is probably the hardest part of my career.

Traveling can be very wearing. People hear that you go to Europe, and hear that you go to this place and that place, and think, "How wonderful it must be." They don't realize that all I get to see are hotel rooms, the airports, and the venues where my concerts are held. But, that's fine with me, after all that's what I'm there to do. It's exhausting, but it's fun.

I love New York. I think it's my favorite place in the world. I'm going to live on Long Island forever, I really think so. To me, Long Island is so real, and there are things to do, but it's not like New York City, where it's too busy, so it's ideal for me.

TELEVISION

Of all of the television shows I've done, I think that being on "American Bandstand" was the most thrilling. It was a big thrill for my mom, too, because she wanted to meet Dick Clark! "American Bandstand" is probably the greatest rock and roll TV show ever. I appeared on the show a few times, and I always looked forward to doing that show.

BOYFRIENDS

I've never really gotten too serious with anyone. I don't feel that I'm really ready for that yet. I just think that maybe I'm too fickle! I'm just your typical, fickle nineteen-year-old! When I have time, I do date. There are a couple of guys I have gone out with for a while, including TV actor Brian Bloom.

I went out with Brian for a while, but I still only saw him like once a month. So, it is kind of hard for me to have any kind of serious relationship now. I went with Brian to my senior prom. We had a good relationship, because we had a lot in common. He has an acting career, and we had a lot of the same thoughts on various things. He wasn't really caught up in that whole celebrity party scene either, so we both enjoyed doing something low-keyed, like going to the movies. But, it just kind of died down, probably because of our schedules.

As opposed to having a steady boyfriend, I'm more into hanging out with my friends. I'm more into being close with people that way, and not anything serious right now. What I do with my career consumes most of my time.

And that's good for me right now. I guess, if I meet Mr. Wonderful right now, I'll make time. If it happens, it happens.

MY FANS

Whenever I meet fans, I can really relate to them, because I'm such a fan of so many people that it's easy for me to understand my fans. Before I had my own records, I was always listening to my favorite radio station, and calling in and requesting songs, and winning contests. I know what it's like to look forward to going to someone's concert, or having to scalp tickets to see someone you are dying to see.

I understand. Let's say someone comes by and knocks on your front door, sure — it's an invasion of privacy — on one hand. But, at the same time, I always say to my mom, "Don't you think that if I was like in London three years ago, and someone tipped me off to where George Michael lived, don't you think that I would have knocked on his door?" I would probably figure, "Well, the worst thing that could happen would be to have him slam the door in my face!" So, I realize the whole feeling of being a fan, and wanting to meet somebody who you look up to.

It is strange, however. Obviously, because I'm just me. I can't envision why people would flip-out if they run into me in a normal situation, like at a store or a restaurant. When I'm up on stage, that's another story — I'm on stage and they're in the audience. That seems natural. But, if I'm just out walking around shopping, it seems odd to have people reacting to the mere sight of me. I understand that I'm a well-known pop singer, but I still feel like a normal teenager.

Recently I was out in public, and I fell down and hurt my knee. I happened to be at a local movie theater, and I was just out for a normal evening. When I slipped and fell, I just got up and kept on walking. These girls came by and said to me, "Are you O.K.?" but they

With choreographer Barry Lather and Denise, on the set of my "Electric Youth" video.

In June of 1989, I filled in for Shadoe Stevens when he took a weeklong vacation from hosting ABC-Radio's "American Top 40."

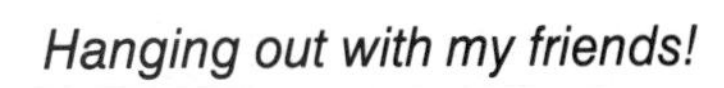

Hanging out with my friends!

At an amusement park in Houston with Dad and Denise.

Iris, Chris, and Deb.

I come from a very affectionate family! That's me with Aunt Linda and Uncle Carl.

At Disney World, age three.

Michele and me.

My favorite outfit!

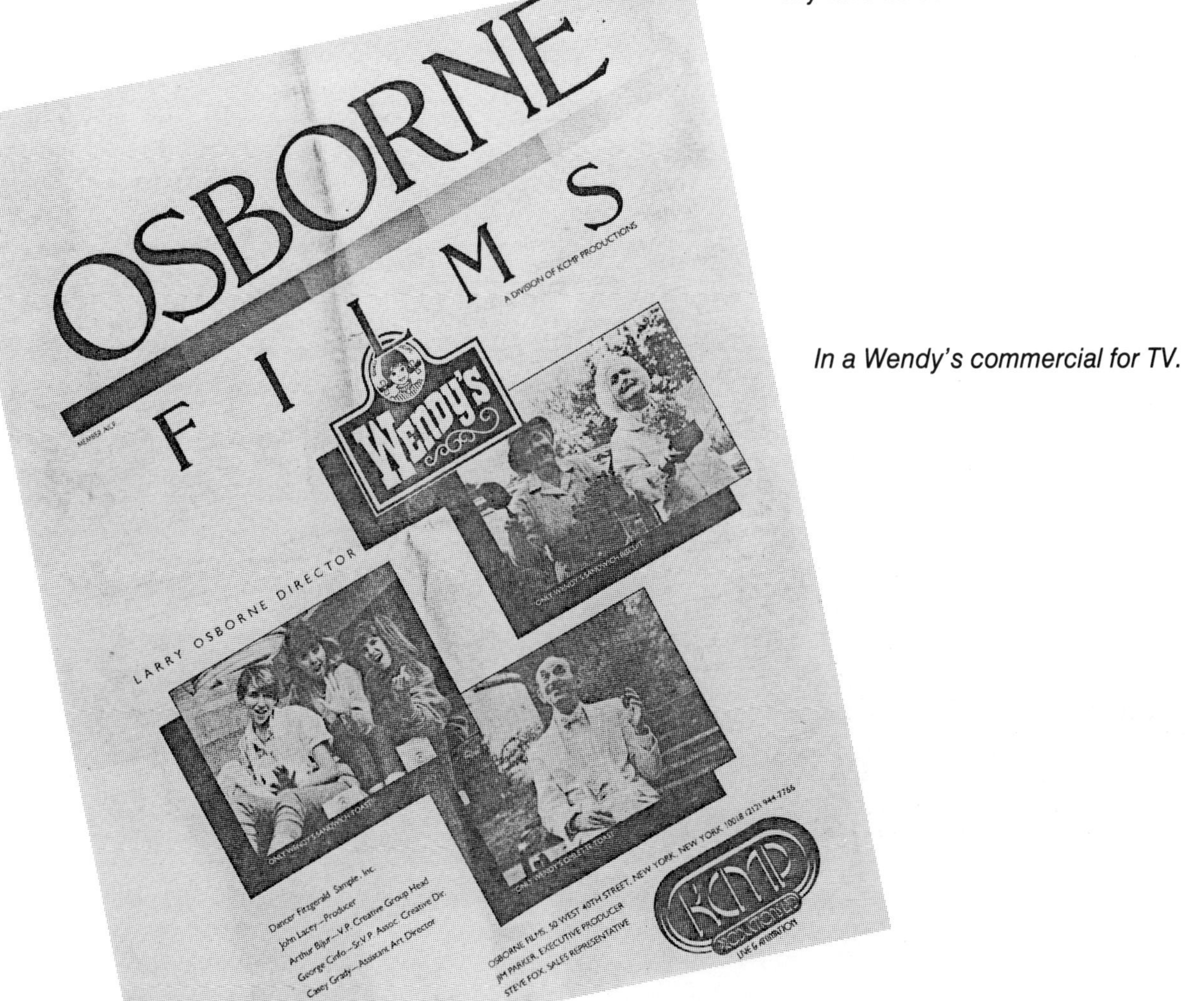

In a Wendy's commercial for TV.

I guess that I have grown since elementary school!

Denise, Debbie, Karen, and Michel at my eighteenth birthday party.

At South Street Seaport on Thanksgiving Day 1987.

didn't see my face. And I replied, "I'm fine," and kept on moving. It would have been a total disaster if I had been recognized. It was at *Ghostbusters II,* and the place was packed with kids. If I just walk around with my head down, no one recognizes me. Anyone who sees me just thinks I'm an average teenage girl, and I'm fine. I just had to make sure that when I fell, I didn't stay down on the ground long enough to be recognized!

MAKE-UP

If I were going to give someone make-up tips, I would have to say, "Keep it natural looking." In school, in ninth and tenth grade, I went through the whole phase of trying to look like everybody else. Everybody does it. But, then in twelfth grade, it's like people suddenly decide to become more individual by that time, because they're not trying to prove anything to anyone anymore.

My making that statement probably isn't going to stop anyone from playing "follow the leader" in ninth or tenth grade, but, at the same time, you should just realize that it's just better to be yourself. If you ask guys what they like in girls, you'll find that they don't like girls who look like clones of one another. I think that, at times, guys are more individual and more casual in school. I think that's the best way to be: go for comfort. That's what I say: Look natural and be comfortable. Who cares what everyone else thinks?

THE HATS

The hats that I wear symbolize "fun" to me. I guess that's why I've always been into them. I don't know, I think that some people

Amid building my "dream house" on Long Island.

Keeping fit in my new workout room.

are just meant to wear hats. They finish off an outfit. They're fun, and I like hats of all kinds. I used to try on big floppy hats, and old fashioned hats, and it's fun for me to change my hats when I change my mood.

The black felt hats that I so often wear have become something of a trademark for me. There is a funny story that goes along with my original black felt hat.

The hats which have an indention in the middle on the top never look right on me. They don't look good on a lot of people; it's hard to make them look good. So, I was doing this radio promotion on a station's morning show, and Michael Damian was there, and he had this black hat on. So I said, "Oh, can I try it on?" He let me try it on, and I wore it through the whole interview, and he said, "Oh, you can keep it." And I said, "No, no, no." And he said, "Yes, yes, yes." So I kept it!

This is my advice about hats: Buy a hat in a big size, then you won't get "hat hair." "Hat hair" is when you wear a hat that crushes your hair, so that when you take off the hat, it looks like you're still wearing it!

Well, this hat that Michael Damian gave to me was really big, and it was perfectly round, with a perfectly round rim. It's still a hat that I wear all of the time. I must have sixty hats in my collection by now. I have tons of them. I have hats with lights, and hats with bows. I even have one with little teddy bears all around the rim. It's the funniest thing! I have fishing hats, I have one that looks like a train conductor's hat. I have all kinds of hats, and I love them all.

DIET AND FITNESS

At the moment I'm on a high energy diet,

so I don't get run down from my hectic schedule. Although I still love junk food, I haven't eaten it for a while. I've been on a "no sugar" diet. I went to a nutritionist for allergies, to see how I was responding to different foods.

When you have an allergic reaction to food, it runs you down, and wears out your immune system. If you are as active as I am, you can't afford to get run down. For two solid years I lived on hamburgers, Chinese food, and pizza. It's easy to get into that rut when you're on the road, or ordering out for food while in the recording studio. That's all I ate, and basically it just caught up to me. I started feeling tired all of the time, and I feel a lot better now.

Now what I do is, I just eat like white meat and vegetables, and brown rice, and rice cakes. It's not as good tasting as pizza — I don't care what anybody says! I'll never totally get used to this new diet. I really only have to be strict about it for three months, and then I can start working some other things into my diet.

I don't think that I'm going to go back to totally eating junk food, though. I just can't afford to do that. You're better off eating real food, than eating junk food which is loaded with salt and sugar. I would have eggs, or a bagel, or a donut for breakfast. Then I had a bagel, a donut and a chocolate milkshake for lunch every day I was in junior high school.

Just as important as eating the right things, I also believe in getting the right amount of exercise. Even though I was eating all of that junk food, I never really gained weight, because I was physically so active. I mean, jumping around on stage, I felt like I lost five pounds during a show! I wasn't obviously, or I'd be a negative weight, but exercise obviously helps. My regular regimen consists mainly of dancing, and jumping around on stage. In the new house that I live in with my parents and my sisters there is an exercise room, with all kinds of Nautalis equipment to work out on, and sometimes I use that to help keep me fit.

Before I go on tour, I start training. I do it for a month before I go out on the road. That keeps my stamina up. But the best workout is still the time I spend on stage. I like to be in tip-top shape when I'm on stage.

MY ROOM

My room is a mess! It's very busy, and it's very fun. In my room, I have posters on the wall — including a virtual shrine to George Michael. Well, it isn't quite to that extreme, but I do have a huge personally autographed poster of him on one of my walls! I also have a Billy Joel poster, and an INXS poster. I have a

d a great time painting this mural on the wall
y bedroom!

whole wall full of hats. I've got a big mural that I've painted on the wall. I worked on it for quite a while. Painting that was my form of relaxation while I was recording my "Electric Youth" album. I would come home and paint on my wall to unwind. I would just turn on all of my Billy Joel records and paint. It felt great!

My bed is covered with a green bedspread, and I have things hanging all over the walls. It's really cluttered. I have a lot of clothes, and they are just thrown everywhere. I'm really messy, but it's organized messy! Anyone who comes into my room wouldn't be able to find anything, but I know where everything is. It goes something like: "The keys to my car are under the shirt that is behind my chair." If someone comes in and "cleans up," I can't find anything!

SONGWRITING

My songs have become more personal to me over the past few years. When I was very young, I'd write about anything at all. But, how much can a five- or a ten-year-old write about? My first song was called "Make Sure You Know Your Classroom." I wrote it about starting kindergarten when I was five years old. I guess I had some kind of subconscious fear about starting school!

I can remember some other songs I wrote when I was about eight, nine, ten . . . "Lovely Day On The Farm" was inspired by a visit to our relatives in New Jersey. "One Of Those Days" was about waking up only to find out there was no hot water for a shower, and my breakfast cereal was soggy.

But, the song that got things rolling was one based on all the places my family and I had vacationed called "I Come From America." Winning the songwriting competition sponsored by radio station WOR really encouraged me to become serious about my writing.

I can remember coming home from school one day and writing a song called "So Sweet The Music." Music was one of the only subjects that I felt comfortable writing about at the age of twelve. In my mind, this was the first "real song" that I wrote. I played it for everyone on the piano. In my opinion, any song that can sound good with just a piano and vocal, and no electronics, is an ageless and a timeless song. Who knows . . . maybe I'll release all of those early songs someday!

I write about every little thing that happens to me. If it's not too exciting — I exaggerate! It's kind of strange to write songs even as a teenager, because my family gives me the third degree about the subjects I write about. That's something no one ever thinks about. I told my mom not to ask me who or what a song is about, to spare me the embarrassment, but she can probably tell anyway! I love writing because it's like keeping a diary. There are some songs that are very personal that haven't been released. For now, I like to record songs with universal themes that everyone can relate to.

I probably come up with some of the weirdest and most honest songs late at night. Your subconscious takes over at three or four o'clock in the morning, and you wake up the next day and wonder, "Did I say that?"

A lot of people think of pop music, especially love songs, as being cliché-ish. If you consider people's everyday lives to be rubbish, then there's something wrong with you!

I have written songs about more serious subject matters, but I don't feel ready to release any of them. It's not that I don't care about what goes on in the world, I just find it all so depressing. Is child abuse, hunger, and violence really something to sing about? I like to write music that allows people to escape a bit and just have fun. If people want to get disgusted by world issues, they can turn on the eleven o'clock news. If they want to hear songs they can relate to on an everyday basis — songs about life — they can tune me in!

MISCONCEPTIONS

Everyone immediately assumes that if you're in the music business, you're conceited. I guess it would be easy to get a swelled head if everything just fell into your lap, but after working in this business for thirteen years, I realize you can't take anything for granted. I admit that I've been lucky in many ways. I'm lucky to have support from my family, and I'm lucky that I had people who were willing to take chances on me. But, believe me — that took a lot of banging on doors, and a lot of proving myself. The bottom line is — I've worked too hard and I've learned too much — so there's no way anyone could ever tell me "no." True, I've been lucky, but there's no such thing as a whole career based on luck. You've got to have something more to back it up.

I'm never purposely obnoxious to people, but I am very strong willed and definite about what I want. After all, it's my life! People will always try to see how hard they can work you, and how much they can get from you. You have to be tuned into these things, and I am. I put 150% into what I do, and I expect the same from everyone I work with. If you let people walk all over you — face it — they will. I know you always see me smiling, and I usually am always smiling, but when someone makes a wrong move relating to my career, I get very defensive, and I definitely speak up about it. I've worked too hard!!!

RELIGION

I've always been religious in the sense that I've always believed in prayer and God. I go to church every Sunday, but if you don't really believe in your religion, it's worthless to go to church. I can remember praying really hard for things, but only a few times. Those prayers were answered, too! I don't pray just when I want things.

My prayers usually consist more of "thank you's" than "give me's." I pray for people who have died, and I know they can hear me. Prayers also help you figure out your priorities. You're not only talking to God, but you're talking to yourself and telling yourself how much you have to be thankful for, and you realize that material things or wishes that seem so important, really are unimportant in the overall picture!

WORK, WORK, WORK

I'm usually involved in every phase of my career. It's definitely a lot of work, but it's more rewarding in the end. I want to present myself honestly to people, and in order to do that, I'm involved in the merchandising, press, videos, clothing, and everything. The only other person I can really trust when it comes to my career is my mom. But, even then, she consults me on every decision. God forbid someone turns down an event I want to participate in, or O.K.'s a photo that I don't like. No one ever hears the end of it!

When it comes to recording my songs, I'm involved in every aspect of that, too. I couldn't imagine spending a week on vocals, walking out of the studio, and calling it "my album."

HONESTY

O.K., so "honesty" is the name of one of my favorite Billy Joel songs, but "honesty" is also something I believe in. I can remember when I was a little girl, and lying awake in bed one night because I told a little white lie. My mom had given me money to buy a souvenir on a class trip to a heliport. We all received free T-shirts, so I treated the class to candy with my money. I didn't know if Mom would approve of this, so I told her I spent the money on the shirt.

At midnight, I went downstairs crying hysterically, "Mom, I have to admit . . . I spent your money on candy for the class, not the shirt!" I just couldn't fall asleep without getting that off my chest. I'm like that to this day. You can sense in a second if I'm lying. I feel stupid lying. I know that I'd be hurt if my family or friends lied to me, so I never lie to anyone about anything! Trust me!

10

Dreams

Everyone has plans and dreams for the future. Some people turn their dreams into reality, and some people just have dreams. I've been fortunate enough to have had several of my dreams come true. The nice thing about dreams, and setting goals for yourself, is that once you accomplish those goals, you can come up with a whole new set of dreams that you want to come true. You should never stop dreaming about things that you want to happen in life. At the moment, the following things are some of my dreams for the future.

One is to do a duet with Billy Joel, and I'd also like to do a song with George Michael someday. My main goal however, is to maintain a comfortable level of success. I never want to have to worry about whether I have a hot single or not. I just always want to know that I'm going to have an audience who will be there for me and that I'll always be able to tour and make albums.

I'd like to write and produce songs for other people. One of the people I will be working with is Keith Stewart, my back-up singer/dancer. I've also written and produced three songs for the pop singer, Ana, for her new album. I really just want to work with people I really believe in, and have a personal interest in — whether they're known or unknown or whatever.

THE "WONDER YEARS" SOUNDTRACK

One of the things that I recently completed, was recording two songs on the "Wonder Years" soundtrack. When a recording was being done for the television show "Wonder Years," the producers asked me to contribute to it. That happens to be my favorite prime time television show, so I was excited to be asked. Karen put that deal together for me. The songs that I recorded will be used on the TV show. I have been approached to act on other television shows, but I wasn't interested at the time. At this point, the only dramatic show or sitcom that I would consider being a guest on is "Wonder Years," because it's a great show. In my opinion, it's the best thing on television at the moment. The two songs that I have recorded for the "Wonder Years" soundtrack are: an original song called "Come Home," and my version of the rock and roll classic "In The Still Of The Night."

"SKIRTS"

My movie career is due to get underway in January 1990. I have signed a motion picture contract with Tri-Star Pictures, which has just merged with Columbia Pictures. The first film that I'm going to make is called *Skirts.*

Kenny Ortega is directing it, and he's the person who put together *Dirty Dancing,* so this should be really exciting for me!

The way that that came about is that we had signed a movie deal some time ago, and then we were just waiting for the right project to come along. I read a lot of scripts and none of them were right for me. This one came along, and it was so "me," and the role was so "me." When this script came around, Columbia set up a meeting with me. I met with Amy Pascal and Barry Sammath of Columbia Pictures, and they said, "We have this project, and we think this is going to be perfect for you." They described it, and I just fell in love with the story.

The character that I play, her name is Betty. She moves from Scarsdale to the Bronx, and she has to totally readjust. It takes place in 1964, the year of the World's Fair in New York City. For me, this is like ideal. Because I said to them, "Oh, my God! If you could see the car that I drive, and hear the kind of music that I listen to — it's totally '50's and '60's!" I'm also going to be involved in the soundtrack album. I have a lot of '50's and '60's sounding songs that I haven't put on any of my albums, because I've been wanting to do a whole project about that era, using that style of music and this is the perfect opportunity.

The film *Skirts* has dancing in it, and even more than that, is the fact that the acting is the focus. I worked with Kenny on the screen test, and I just loved working with him. I think that the chemistry was "right" there. I really worked hard the week that I did the screen test. And, it felt great! When I was done with those scenes, I felt like they went well. I mean, just the idea of performing and accomplishing something, for me feels great, no matter what it is. Because I've done some acting before, which a lot of people don't really know, it's like getting back to something that I have done, but now I'm going to do it in a bigger way. The whole project really appeals to me. At the end of that day of the screen test, I felt that things came out of me that had never come out of me before. I was just really excited by the whole experience.

The funniest part was, that there was this one scene where there is that tension, where the characters are almost going to kiss, and they don't. My cousin Sal was watching the screen test, and afterward he said, "Oh, my God! I thought you were really going to kiss, and I thought that I was going to have to grab that guy by the throat. I really felt like I was at the movies, and that was the cliffhanger!" That was such an honest response, and I just said "Yes! That scene felt great!"

I had to go off my diet for the scene. I had to eat a canole — but I lived. It was a tough job, but somebody had to do it! I broke out the chocolate covered canole for the last take. (But, the original ones are better — in my opinion!) Canoles are the best.

When the film goes into production, we may shoot some of it in New York, but most of it is going to be filmed in L.A. That means I am going to have to be in Los Angeles for a while, which will be really weird. It's kind of scary, because I've never lived anyplace else but here on Long Island. But, I'll get used to it. I'll be on the movie set all day, so it will be fun.

Another one of my goals is to someday get married and have a family. This will be later on down the road. That's surprising in a way, because these days a lot of people say, "Oh, I don't want to get married." I definitely do want to get married . . . someday.

I definitely see myself staying in show business. I want to continue to juggle all the different aspects of the entertainment world: records, videos, movies, television, and concerts. I want to have it all!

I don't think that my working in movies is going to change who I am. Even though I will be starring in a movie, I don't think of myself as a "movie star." Some people will say to me, "Why don't you buy this or that, or why don't you do this or that." And I say, "When I'm really rich, I'll go do that." And they say to me, "But you are rich and famous!" But I still

Debbie Gibson

ELECTRIC YOUTH WORLD TOUR

ON SALE TOM'W 9 AM!

SPECIAL GUESTS:

PRESENTED BY Natural Wonder COSMETICS

SEPTEMBER 21 • 8 PM

ALL SEATS RESERVED $20. AVAILABLE AT MADISON SQUARE GARDEN BOX OFFICE, OR CALL TO CHARGE BY PHONE: 212-307-7171

Produced by Ron Delsener

ATLANTIC

madison square garden

A Paramount Communications Company

can't believe it myself. I know there are people who know who I am, but there are still so many more who don't even know who I am. I think of that, more than I think of myself as being famous.

I ran into a guy in an elevator in England, and I was wearing a George Michael T-shirt, and this guy didn't even know who George Michael was! That just goes to show you that you have to keep everything in perspective. Fame is only of value to a certain degree. There are more important things than being famous. I don't think my career success has affected me that way at all.

I think to myself, "I'm not cool enough to be famous!" And I definitely hate the word "star." To me it has a real negative connotation. The only thing that I like about the word "star," is that it makes me think of "confidence." To me someone who is a star just has an aura about them that makes people want to watch them and everything. I like that element of the term, but I also think of "arrogance" and being snooty going along with that word, as well. That's part of the word "star" that can be eliminated. I never want to have that stuck-up attitude, or have people think of me in that way.

More than being a star, I really want to be a creative and successful entertainer. That's basically it.

With my ASCAP Award for songwriting. I tied with Bruce Springsteen as Songwriter of the Year!

Discography

ALBUMS:

(1) **OUT OF THE BLUE** (Atlantic Records 1987)

- "Out Of The Blue"
  Produced by Fred Zarr & Deborah Gibson
- "Staying Together"
  Produced by Fred Zarr & Deborah Gibson
- "Only In My Dreams"
  Produced by Fred Zarr
- "Foolish Beat"
  Produced by Deborah Gibson
- "Red Hot"
  Produced by John Morales & Sergio Munzibai
- "Wake Up To Love"
  Produced by Fred Zarr & Deborah Gibson
- "Shake Your Love"
  Produced by Fred Zarr
- "Fallen Angel"
  Produced by Fred Zarr
- "Play The Field"
  Produced by Lewis A. Martinee
- "Between The Lines"
  Produced by John Morales & Sergio Munzibai

(2) **ELECTRIC YOUTH** (Atlantic Records 1989)

- "Who Loves Ya Baby?"
  Produced by Fred Zarr & Deborah Gibson
- "Lost In Your Eyes"
  Produced by Deborah Gibson
- "Love In Disguise"
  Produced by Deborah Gibson
- "Helplessly In Love"
  Produced by Deborah Gibson
- "Silence Speaks (A Thousand Words)"
  Produced by Deborah Gibson
- "Should've Been The One"
  Produced by Deborah Gibson

- "Electric Youth"
  Produced by Fred Zarr
- "No More Rhyme"
  Produced by Fred Zarr
- "Over The Wall"
  Produced by Deborah Gibson
- "We Could Be Together"
  Produced by Fred Zarr & Deborah Gibson
- "Shades Of The Past"
  Produced by Fred Zarr

(3) **FATAL BEAUTY** Soundtrack Album (Atlantic Records 1988)

- "Red Hot"
  Produced by John Morales & Sergio Munzibai

(4) **WONDER YEARS** Soundtrack Album (Atlantic Records 1989)

- "Come Home"
  Produced by Deborah Gibson
- "In The Still Of The Night"
  Produced by Deborah Gibson

SINGLES:

(1) "Only In My Dreams"
(2) "Shake Your Love"
(3) "Out Of The Blue"
(4) "Foolish Beat"
(5) "Staying Together"
(6) "Lost In Your Eyes"
(7) "Electric Youth"
(8) "No More Rhyme"
(9) "We Can Be Together"

With Doug Morris of Atlantic Records and my mom, on my eighteenth birthday.

With Dad and Mom at the ASCAP Awards.

Electric Youth!

Denise, Debbie, Karen, and Michele.

Two wild and crazy guys: my publicist David Salidor and my co-author Mark Bego.

My Green Machine!

Chythia Rhodes, me, and Richard Marx at the Grammy Awards, 1988.

Lounging in L.A.

With Ahmet Ertegun, President of Atlantic Records.

Mom and I behind our Foster Grants!